D1479097

Inside German Communism

Rosa Leviné-Meyer

INSIDE GERMAN COMMUNISM

Memoirs of Party Life
in the Weimar Republic

edited and introduced by
David Zane Mairowitz

Pluto  Press

First published 1977
by Pluto Press Limited
Unit 10 Spencer Court,
7 Chalcot Road,
London NW1 8LH

Copyright © Pluto Press 1977

ISBN 0 904383 34 2

Typeset by Preface Limited, Salisbury
Printed by The Camelot Press Limited, Southampton

Designed by Richard Hollis GrR
and David King

Contents

Editor's Introduction

Rosa Leviné-Meyer's memoirs, written in English nearly half a century after the events described, span the entire experience of early German Communism from the formation of the Spartakusbund to the Stalinisation of the KPD. Married successively to two important Communist Party leaders, herself a participant in the events, Rosa Leviné-Meyer's approach is both personal and political, taking us through the daily life of the KPD from the viewpoint of a rank-and-file member who is nonetheless within earshot of the top leadership.

Born in the Russian ghetto town of Grodek in 1890, the daughter of a rabbi, Rosa Leviné-Meyer's formal education ended at the age of 11, giving way after that to a life-long obsession with self-teaching. At the age of 20 she went to Germany to work as a governess, in order to learn the language. It was there she met Eugen Leviné, himself a Russian emigre in Heidelberg.

Rosa Leviné-Meyer's political education was virtually non-existent until thrust upon her by the insurrectionary events of 1917–19, by the inspirational proximity of two extraordinary husbands and by personal exposure to revolutionary personalities including Luxemburg, Liebknecht, Radek, Bukharin, Muenzenberg, Zetkin, Zinoviev, Lenin, Trotsky. In 1915 she married Leviné who, four years later, led the short-lived Soviet Republic in Munich, was captured and executed by firing squad. The author has already told this story in an earlier volume, *Leviné: The Life of a Revolutionary* (Saxon House / Pluto Press 1973), which carries her life up to 1920. The present memoir follows directly from the death of Leviné (which was, concurrently, the end of the German Revolution). As Rosa Leviné revives her shattered private life, so too the young Communist Party struggles to build on a vehement revolutionary birth which resulted, nonetheless, in failure. One of its most important, though least known, new leaders is Ernst Meyer and, in the aura of his political fate, culminating in premature death in 1930, Rosa Leviné (Leviné-Meyer by 1922) continues her own journey into Communism.

Once again the author holds up a mirror representing the German movement and casts a personal image there. If the relationship with the fiery Leviné is shown amidst assassinations, mass demonstrations, the White terror, so the new Party compulsion to take stock and create a strong foundation afterwards is reflected in her marriage with the more retiring, though no less active Meyer. The distinction between political methods, as between the character of each husband, is also the variation in content from the first book to the present one. *Leviné* is essentially a political romance, ending in violent barricades and emotionally fraught prison cells. Rosa Leviné-Meyer's account of the 1920–33 events is more subdued, the accent always placed on more sober, often insufferably dull, though revealing, committee-meetings and conferences, as well as on the character of Ernst Meyer, more a focus for the political attitudes of others than a leader of authority in his own right.

The memoirs of Rosa Leviné-Meyer, while concentrating on factional squabbles, still show the Communist Party at a time when it was the only real hope for swift and decisive social change. That she is able to relate this core of optimism while documenting the encroachment of Stalinism and accompanying capitulation of the German Party, sets her memoir apart from countless others, from many countries, whose entire form and purpose is the revelation of betrayal and bitterness. With her constant journeying between Germany and Soviet Russia it is impossible not to be aware, behind her warnings and disappointments, of the thrill and promise of Bolshevism, the likes of which we will hardly experience again in our own time.

After continuing to hold illegal meetings, under an assumed name, Rosa Leviné-Meyer finally escaped Nazi Germany in May 1933, through the Czech border. She then fled to Paris where she intended to join Trotsky's opposition group. Having recently returned from the Soviet Union, she was asked by Trotsky's son to write an article for the exiles' bulletin. Asking whether she could state that Trotsky's following inside Russia was very small, she was rebuffed and became disillusioned. Disheartened also by the People's Front and by Comintern policy in France, she came to England in October 1934, where she has lived ever since. During the early years she spoke at Party cells of German refugees in London and during the 1960s gave two political lectures at Oxford. But her major contribution has been as a source of private political discussion for historians and activists. Guests for tea and politics have included, over the years, Eric Hobsbawm, Hermann Weber and Isaac Deutscher (who first encouraged her to write her memoirs). She has also had theoretical correspondence with the above, as well as with Herbert Marcuse and others. Younger leftists who have come to learn from and debate with her include Rudi Dutschke and Daniel Cohn-Bendit.

Rosa Leviné-Meyer has consistently retained her strong political independence from all Left factions and, along with her two books, has been writing a lengthy indictment of Trotsky over the past few years. Despite the absence of strong revolutionary context and her general pessimism with regard to the world Communist movement, she holds to her belief that a revolutionary situation exists and needs, first of all, a true Communist Party to spur it on.

Now in her mid-eighties, Mrs Leviné-Meyer has been unable to participate directly in the initial selection of this material from her original manuscript, which is approximately twice its current length. With her approval it has been edited down to reveal the basic narrative of the memoirs, while a great deal of theoretical opinion, not especially relevant to the English edition, has been cut. There have also been necessary stylistic changes and clarification of time sequence through the re-shuffling of sections, but all first-hand documentary material and the through-line of the author's political conviction have been faithfully retained.

Wherever possible first hand source material, translated by the author from original documents, has been double-checked. It has not been possible to do so for the following:

Ernst Meyer's reaction to the Zinoviev letter and the ECCI's response to him;

Ernst Meyer's 1925 note concerning Scholem et al.;

Ernst Meyer's note to Rosa Leviné-Meyer on his way to the 1927 Conference;

Ernst Meyer's letters to the Politbureau of 28 November 1927 and 19 December 1928;

Material relating to the Centre Group and the 1924 Congress in Chapter 7;

Material relating to the Third Period in Chapter 18.

I would like to thank the following people for their help on this project: Hanne Marschall of the Bundesarchiv, Koblenz and Professor Dr Hermann Weber for providing historical documentation; Pete Burgess for checking translations of original German material; and Richard Kuper for writing the historical introduction which follows.

D.Z.M.

Historical Note

Formed at the end of 1918 when Karl Liebknecht and Rosa Luxemburg took the Spartakusbund out of the Independent Social Democratic Party, the Communist Party of Germany (KPD) remained a small and relatively isolated sect for almost two years. Many of its leading figures – Luxemburg, Liebknecht, and Leo Jogiches among them – were murdered by the mercenary soldiers of the *Freikorps* which the new Social Democratic government was using to stem the revolutionary tide in 1919. But then at the Halle Congress in October 1920 a majority of the Independents voted to joint the Communist International and a new united Communist Party of Germany was formed – a mass party with powerful sections of workers affiliated to it.

The new party was faced with the same problem that had plagued the early Communist Party – how to bridge the gulf between small, restless, aggressive, quasi-utopian sections of workers and intellectuals who wanted socialism and who wanted it now, and the mass of the working class.

The party was perpetually engaged in trying to curb its extreme left wing, to impose a disciplined, patient approach on this semi-anarchistic insurrectionary section. As early as 1919 a large section of the Communist Party had split off 'to the left', to form the short-lived Communist Workers Party of Germany (KAPD), in protest at what they saw as the KPD's opportunism. Again in 1921 the restless pressure for immediate success surfaced and led the KPD into the so-called March Action, a call to insurrection to protest at the provocative military occupation of the Mansfeld area, in the hope that heroic leadership could provoke the masses into revolutionary activity. The disastrous failure of this 'offensive theory' lost the KPD a great deal in membership and influence. It also provoked its first major leadership crisis – Paul Levi, who had bitterly opposed the March Action, was expelled for the way in which his criticisms had been made.

A period of retrenchment and construction began, effectively led by Ernst Meyer who became Chairman of the Politbureau. The KPD now turned against the putschist image they had created and attempted, through united front work, to build up Communist credibility in the eyes of social democratic workers. Following the assassination of Foreign Minister Rathenau on 24 June 1922 in which sections of the police and the military were involved, the KPD called for united workers' action and three days later the Berlin Accord was adopted by representatives of the five major labour and trade union organisations (the Communists, the Independents, the Social Democrats, and the two major federations of trade union and employee associations). In the event the SPD's commitment to the bourgeois parties proved once again stronger than its support for a straight class grouping in defence of workers' interests and the Accord foundered. But the KPD had made real gains in membership and influence.

Even now, however, the tensions within the Party were acute. The left-wing, perhaps a third of the Party, were critical of the united front activity. Many of them opposed the policy as such. They were excluded from the new Central Committee elected in January 1923, although Ernst Meyer, against whom they had directed so much of their venom, was dropped as a concession to them. In May, a few of the left were readmitted onto the Central Committee in deference to the wishes of the Communist International but the divisions remained. The left accused the Brandler-led Central Committee of passivity, opportunism and revisionism; and indeed Brandler was mesmerised by the need to win over the workers as they were, reformist illusions and all. For its part the left fell back onto the old positions which had characterised all the left-wing groupings since the Party's formation – a desire for revolutionary and offensive action independent of real possibilities, an unwillingness to face up to problems of transition and, above all, a polemical style of bitter, personal vituperation directed at the incumbent leadership.

The KPD barely responded to the crises of 1923: the French occupation of the Ruhr, the galloping inflation and the virtual paralysis of the central government. They had no clear strategy and no appreciation of the obvious revolutionary possibilities. It was not until September that a decision was taken to make a bid for power using Communist strength in Saxony and Thuringia as a base. At the end of September the army commander General Mueller had ordered the workers' militias in Saxony to be disbanded: the Zeigner government refused. On 10 October Brandler entered the Zeigner government, a Social-Democratic government dependent on KPD support, forming a 'government of proletarian defence'. The KPD hoped this would give the workers access to arms and make Saxony a proletarian bastion in central Germany. Likewise with Thuringia where Communists entered the government a few days later. As the crisis deepened the army was ordered to depose these two State governments. The KPD decided to call for a general strike and to launch an armed struggle: 23 October had already been set as the date for insurrection. But at the Chemnitz Conference of factory councils on 21 October it became clear that there would be no mass support. The KPD's earlier refusals to join the State governments and the sudden reversal had only caused confusion. Brandler's vacillation and indeed his leadership throughout 1923 now took its toll. His appeal for support at Chemnitz fell on stony ground and the next day the insurrection was called off.

The high point of the crisis had passed in September with the fall of the Cuno government. Since then, the formation of a grand coalition government under Gustav Stresemann, the ending of passive resistance to the French occupation, the stabilisation of the mark, had provided a framework for a new period of capitalist stability. When the KPD finally awoke to the new reality, it had to face the problems of building a revolutionary party in a non-revolutionary situation.

The debate over the responsibility for the October debacle coincided with the first overt signs of a leadership struggle in Russia. The German party's failure to evolve a settled, accepted and stable leadership was now to weigh heavily, for the Russian factions were in search of allies.

Matters came to a head at the Ninth Congress of the KPD in Frankfurt in 1924. The failure of Brandler's policies led to a complete sweep of the old leadership from office. The left, headed by Ruth Fischer and Arkadi Maslow, now came to power.

It was to be a short-lived triumph. By April 1925 the Comintern line had changed. It now recognised that capitalism had achieved a temporary stabilisation, that there was a need to win over social-democratic workers, and that the left who so recently had gained control over the Party machine should be broken. In July the ECCI delegates to the Tenth KPD Congress attacked the ultra-left wing, led by Rosenberg and Scholem, as 'part of the international fraction against bolshevism'. At first the Party refused to disown them, and re-elected them to the Central Committee. But the ECCI intervened again. A KPD delegation was summoned to Moscow and, after private discussions, an open letter – the so-called Zinoviev Letter – was sent to all organisations and members of the KPD. It mercilessly identified errors of the German party, but concluded that 'it is not the German left which is bankrupt, but a few of its leaders.' On 31 October, at a special conference convened to discuss Zinoviev's 'Open Letter' to the KPD, Fischer and Maslow were disowned for sectarianism, neglect of trade union work, and underhand fighting against the Comintern, by 217 votes to 30, and Thaelmann's 'workers' group' was installed at the head of the Party. Thaelmann and his supporters had always been part of the left within the Party, but this loyal 'proletarian' left was now distinguished from the intellectual Fischer-Maslow left. Zinoviev had succeeded in using an alliance between this loyal left and the older Centre grouping, led by Ernst Meyer, first against the ultra-left and then against Fischer and Maslow.

A more serious and stable policy seemed to result. The Party grew in influence and membership. But in reality, the struggles had been concerned above all to forge a *loyal* leadership, rather than a *leadership*, with the result that events in Russia and the International, the formation of a united left in Russia, Zinoviev's alliance with Trotsky, and Stalin's triumph first against the left opposition and then against the right – swamped it.

Early in 1928 the 'line' changed anew. The principal danger was now seen to be on the right: the Centre Group in Germany were branded as part of the discredited right-wing Brandlerists and hounded from office. With the honourable exception of Ernst Meyer they capitulated and were finally broken in 1929. From then on no fraction or legal opposition was tolerated within the KPD. The Stalinisation of the Party was complete.

The Party was able to enter its final phase, in which social democracy was equated with fascism, as a unified monolith. The leftism which had plagued it throughout the 1920s – the attempts to short-circuit the process of revolutionary development, the impatience which Lenin had campaigned against in 1920 with his attacks on 'left-wing communism' – was given its head.

The KPD marched blindfold to the precipice. On 9 January 1933 Thaelmann spoke enthusiastically of the complete unity of the Party: something as disastrous as October 1923 could never happen again. By the end of the month the Nazis were in power and the final moves for the destruction of German communism were set in train.

1.

The Party After Munich

After the debacle of the Munich Soviet Republic, culminating in June 1919 with the execution of my husband, Eugen Leviné, I was expelled from Bavaria. My first stop was Heidelberg. I was ill with an old complaint, severely aggravated by my shattered nerves. I spent many weeks in hospital, and several months recuperating in the spa town of Duerrheim. My mother-in-law had promised her son that she would stand by me, but there was no place for me in the fixed pattern of her life.

Early in 1920, I moved to Berlin, this time into a home of my own, even though I had to share it with an old friend, the painter Karl-Jakob Hirsch. I had my child with me, and I tried to rebuild my broken life.

The summer of 1920 was a time when Russian delegates started pouring into Germany, to meet the West, to learn – and to convert. I was invited to translate at conferences and private meetings and met some of the chief architects of the Russian Revolution. One was the legendary Artem-Sergeev who had performed acts of rare bravery during the Revolution and become a special favourite of Lenin's. He had defied torture and bullets, but died very soon in a silly accident. After Sergeev's death, Lenin found time to pay a visit to his widow. She was a foolish, hysterical girl, whom I happened to know well, as we had once lived in the same little Russian town. She was from a bourgeois family, but had somehow got mixed up with the Revolution. Lenin must have guessed that she was shunned in her new surroundings, and wanted to set an example of comradeship to the wife of a great revolutionary and the son he had left behind. Moscow remembered that visit for a long time and, needless to say, she was well provided for.

My own favourite was a textile worker, Lebedev, a giant of a Russian with clear blue eyes, in which all his pure upright nature was reflected. He had spent himself in heroic service to the Revolution and died of heart failure in his early forties. We sometimes travelled together outside Berlin, the most memorable journey being to Cottbus, with its large textile industry. The local trade unionists went out of their way to show political tolerance, arranging a meeting to hear what the Bolshevik had to tell them about Russian life, and also to show him a German factory. The factory bosses had apparently decided to prevent any contact with the workers and we were accompanied by managerial staff. This only raised our prestige with the workers who cheered and applauded and tried to shake hands; after all, a textile worker like themselves was being honoured by their bosses.

At the end we were taken for a 'snack' by the factory owner. The table was beautifully laid with exquisite food and drink. My heart sank. We had often been the object of public attention in restaurants when Lebedev was seen cheerfully eating from his knife. We sat down. Lebedev took a sandwich and ate it in the perfect German manner with knife and fork. I nearly embraced him. I did not want this wonderful man to be looked down upon – nor the Bolsheviks generally, for that matter. Lebedev finished his sandwich, took a sip from his glass – 'thank you!' He could not be persuaded to take another bite, however much they tried. 'I do not wine and dine with such people. We have nothing in common', he explained later. 'I just avoided being demonstrative or rude, that's enough.'

Some of the heads of the Communist Party, and their wives, were normally invited to official receptions at the Soviet Embassy. We rubbed shoulders there with the diplomatic corps and other dignitaries of the West and could see them at close quarters.

They used to storm the richly-laden tables like famished tramps. They forgot that they despised their hosts, particularly in the first years of the Revolution, as bandits and half-savages. It became a habit with me to compare 'us' and 'them'. We must never lag behind them in matters of human dignity and I was always deeply alarmed when we did – Lebedev decidedly stood the test.

I met Lozovsky who achieved great notoriety during the second world war as a propaganda chief, a kind of Russian Goebbels, and who was executed by Stalin in the aftermath of the war. I was appointed his private interpreter and we spent a great deal of time together. He was a blacksmith, a very unusual occupation for a Jew, and looked as stalwart and unbending as a man of that trade is expected to be. But he was also a dreamer and his eyes would sometimes grow quite starry, as he spoke of the happy future, when the human race would be freed from hardship and bondage. Like all the top figures of the Russian Revolution, he was a great reader. The speed with which he learnt German was dazzling – he was pushing me out of a job. Within days he was able to understand his many visitors, at least to grasp the gist of the conversation, and even make short replies.

The autumn of 1920 was also the start of my intimate friendship – later leading to marriage – with Ernst Meyer. I first met him in 1917 at Sonya Liebknecht's when he was a married man with two children, and I the wife of Leviné. We had hardly exchanged a word.

In 1918 after the Russian Revolution, I used to see him daily at Rosta, the predecessor of the Tass news agency, when Ernst was the head of the German section, Leviné the Russian section, and I his private secretary.

In contrast to Leviné, who paid no attention to his appearance, Ernst Meyer was always well-groomed, his hair always tidy, his hands manicured – he hardly looked like a revolutionary. But he was a man of great integrity. He voluntarily declined half his salary from Rosta, on the grounds that he only spent half his time working there. Leviné was deeply impressed.

Years later, on my return to Berlin, I was advised that, in any contact with the Party, I should try to approach Ernst Meyer, as the most sympathetic and compassionate of its leaders. We met several times, but the ice between us was only broken on the eve of his departure for Soviet Russia in July 1920. For the first time, we exchanged a few personal words, and we realised how much we really understood each other. We parted with one solitary goodbye kiss, but we both knew that we were now tied to each other.

At the end of 1920, I went to Koenigsberg to join Ernst Meyer, who had been recently removed from the Central Committee, allegedly for 'Right deviations'. I do not recollect the issue, and there are no clear records to judge from, but I do not think it is partiality on my side to attribute his removal to intrigues and factional fights. Lenin, who watched the activities of the German Party very closely and had much opportunity to observe Ernst Meyer during their collaboration on the famous 21 Points (for the admission of the USPD, the 'Independents' into the Comintern), had great confidence in him. It was Lenin's implicit wish that Ernst should lead the forthcoming Congress at which the USPD would merge with the Communists. This was something which Ernst, in his modesty, told me only shortly before his death.

After his removal he was assigned to go to Koenigsberg to organise the publication of a Communist paper (*Echo of the East*). He promised me a Russian section in the paper, but no bait was necessary. I would have gone on any terms. I followed him with my five-year-old boy.

The limited number of Communist leaders was out of proportion to the new requirements. The top strata were too set, too comfortable to give leadership to rebelling masses. One had only to glance at their homes, meet their wives, and go to their coffee parties to grasp how deeply-rooted they were in the middle-class way of life and its traditions. The Communist Party had to draw from the fringe of workers outside the organised parties. A phalanx of smart, gifted youngsters, full of drive, the best intentions and courage, but lacking political experience and links with the working-class movement, penetrated the Party. They filled a glaring hole and, at a stroke, achieved leading positions and notoriety. This is how people like Heinz Neumann, Gerhart Eisler and Ruth Fischer (the most gifted of them all, and only in her mid-twenties) came to exercise such influence over the German revolutionary movement, and to a degree sway its destiny.

No revolution can do without such elements. They are both the strength and weakness of the movement – for they are the chief source of premature actions.

The German workers as a whole were losing patience with their parties and looking for new leadership. To win over the level-headed and experienced workers – the type of men who could be found in the old organisations, the USPD and SPD, became a matter of life and death. The main obstacle to attracting such men into the Communist Party was the behaviour of the Party's own firebrands. Despite their courage and devotion to the cause they alienated the masses by their semi-anarchistic practices. They needed to be purged, and this required long tactful persuasion. But nobody had any use for patience in those days.

The Heidelberg Congress of October 1919 was typical of this impatient mood. Its main purpose was to shake off those Party members who stood in the way of unification with the Independent Social Democratic Party, and of winning the favour of its leaders. It was conducted by Paul Levi, then leader of the Communist Party, perhaps the most impatient of them all. His lordly manner, his haughty disregard for the intellectually inferior, frightened away a great number of people who could have been relied on to become the stalwarts of the revolution, and was the root cause of all the tragic turbulence and the ultimate disintegration of Communism in Germany. For instead of being persuaded, these elements were simply expelled from the Party, and in 1920 formed a party of their own, the 'Communist Workers' Party' (KAPD), in opposition to any 'domination from above', any leadership. Although the new party didn't last long its members did not disappear. Keen revolutionaries at heart, they flocked wherever disturbances broke out, lending them their own chaotic stamp, with acts of adventurism, sometimes bordering on sheer criminality, performed in the name of the Communist Party. These elements were the source of numbers and strength of the later 'Left', under Ruth Fischer and Maslow in Berlin. Lenin tried to win them over and wrote – amidst the sound and fury of a civil war – his masterpiece of political tactics: 'Left-Wing Communism – an Infantile Disorder', for their edification. He also pressed for the Communist Workers' Party to be admitted to the Third International. But after their bitter experience of Heidelberg they trusted no-one.

Our departure from Koenigsberg came quite unexpectedly. Ernst received a telegram at the beginning of 1921, asking him to return immediately to Berlin to take over the leadership of the Party. He had been deposed from the Central Committee for 'Right deviations'. Now he was called back to head a policy which was dangerously close to ultra-leftism, culminating, only a few short weeks later, in the notorious 'March Action'. Nothing could better expose the artificiality of the attacks on Ernst Meyer – and also Ernst's inability to parry them.

'The German revolutionary movement is unthinkable without Ernst Meyer', a Swiss comrade, Rosa Grimm, once said. I thought it was flattery, but events proved that there was never a smoothly-functioning Communist Party without him.

2.   March Action, 1921

After the fusion with the Independent Social Democratic Party (USPD) in October 1920, the Communists reached at a stroke the long-coveted status of a 'Mass-Party'. They now felt compelled to produce results. The influx of some 400,000 to 500,000 new members fostered the illusion that agitation on a local level would arouse the latent discontent which was still very strong among the workers, leading to nation-wide action. The early period of the German revolution had left the Communists with the feeling that 'we just missed it'. It was, they felt, the vacillating of treacherous leaders in the USPD that always restrained the workers from the last victorious battle. Now the masses would follow the Communists' lead if the circumstances of former days could be re-created.

Needless to say, there were enough inflammatory situations in Germany of the early 1920s. In the Mansfeld coal region of Central Germany there were incessant skirmishes between miners and Prussian police detachments. The expectation that the hated Reichswehr would reinforce the police, in order to pacify the district, kept the workers in a state of constant tension. The Party assumed that the Mansfeld unrest would spread if the workers could be aroused by Communist propaganda and examples of revolutionary courage – the so-called 'Offensive Theory'. The immediate task was to set the workers into motion and drive them on by a succession of revolutionary actions. But the 'Offensive Theory' came as a bolt from the blue. There was no mounting revolutionary tide, no mass movement, only a resolution from the top agreed by the Central Committee. The propaganda was accordingly vague and abstract and I, for one, did not grasp where it was leading. The first struggle happened in my own home, between me and my husband – a battle for clarification. It did not occur to me that this in itself showed up the weakness of the new policy – not every Party member had at his disposal a member of the Politbureau for information. I was a good testing ground: if the motives and urgency remained unclear to me, they could not be clear to the workers either. It is amazing that his revolutionary fervour made Ernst blind to this simple fact.

The real struggle occurred in and around Mansfeld where the workers went into action with great courage. It could not be called a 'revolutionary offensive' though, rather a defensive struggle against the Security Police and the Reichswehr detachments. The fight lasted several days. It was distinguished by the arrival of Max Hoelz, a legendary figure of revolutionary Germany, whose bravery caught the imagination of the workers.

The 'Revolutionary Offensive' however, proved a pitifully isolated affair. The country remained mute. The Communist press tried to boost the campaign with vile abuse of the 'treacherous socialist leaders' and thundering appeals to the workers, commanding furious appeals, more like threats: 'The blood of the victims will fall not only on the heads of your leaders but also on your own heads', or by true war declarations: 'He who is not with us is against us!' which of course did not improve matters.

What followed belongs to the ugliest chapters of Communist history. To keep the fire burning the Party resorted to sabotage, bomb-throwing, and outright provocation. Attempts were even made to provoke the Security Police to attack first, so that the workers would start moving. Unemployed workers were formed into storm-brigades, to force their way into factories and try to stop work. Many even carried hand grenades. Even after the fiasco was complete, clashes and brawls were engineered as a means of skilful retreat. It did not seem to matter whose blood would flow. Casualties mounted, but no one dared call off the action for fear of appearing weak and un-revolutionary. In Berlin the Party demanded a strike at all costs and, in obedience, loyal Communists walked out while factories continued working. Their sacrifice only served the factory bosses, providing an opportunity to get rid of the rebels.

The results were devastating. For a long time the anti-Communist press was able to serve up accounts of cloak-and-dagger chaos and unrest. *Vorwaerts*, the SPD paper, even reported the discovery of a cholera-bacteria breeding centre for spreading epidemics. Even allowing for gross exaggeration, there was enough compromising evidence to cause bewilderment and revulsion. And the courts were sending misguided workers to prison by the hundreds.

It is true that even the fiercest critics, such as Paul Levi, admitted there was a difference between what was ordered by the Party, or even known to it, and what actually happened. On the other hand, Ernst Meyer laughed off many of the events which actually took place – they were utterly unknown to him. A violent inner-Party struggle broke out, and the March Action was denounced as a Russian scheme to divert attention of their own workers from their difficulties.

Paul Levi came out with a blood and thunder cry against the invasion of the Party by 'Turkestaners'. He gave the signal by openly condemning the Party. Many leaders, particularly from the former USPD, resigned by the score. The dissolution of the Party seemed complete. But the Leftists had learned nothing. We met Arkadi Maslow on one of our rare weekends outside Berlin. He was returning from Moscow where the Third Comintern Congress had just come to an end, and he reported very vividly of Lenin's dealings with the March Action and with Paul Levi. 'Friendly slaps at Levi, and heavy blows at us', he repeated in consternation. He seemed baffled: so much revolutionary fervour and no thanks; it was unfair . . .

Ernst was thoughtful but at that stage had not fully assessed his mistakes. He was still trying to justify the 'audacity of the attack'. As he wrote in a personal letter in March 1922: 'Just one year ago the worst part of the March rebellion was in progress. Those days haunt me like a nightmare. It was a deadly, daring attack. I would not have missed the experience. Any individual or party which succeeds in surviving such events becomes immune to even the gravest emergency.'*

*On another occasion in Moscow in the late autumn of 1922, when Trotsky heavily criticised the March events, Ernst listened with the air of an outsider whom Trotsky's criticism hardly touched. By then he had completely outgrown his mistakes through his own practical work, the only way one can really overcome political errors. This is why Ernst was such an enemy of 'declarations' of self-criticism.

3.   The Rathenau Affair

These were the conditions under which Ernst Meyer took over the Party leadership. Characteristically, few of the chroniclers of German Communism have mentioned his name or were even aware that from February 1921 to the Leipzig Party Congress of January 1923 Ernst was the Chairman of the Politbureau – in present terms *the* leader of the Party. He carried it through all its crises with a minimum loss of members and prestige, always present where decomposition was strongest, on occasion splitting up tightly knit groups by transplanting members to different localities and to other activities, thus giving them a chance to cool off.

He took on the heavy burden of restoring confidence and putting the Party on its feet, and his efforts brought astonishing results. Even Ruth Fischer, his political opponent, pays him tribute in her book, *Stalin and German Communism*: 'In the second half of 1922 the Party was gaining in numbers and influence. In the third quarter of 1922 it had 218,555 members. It shows a sharp rise from the 180,443 of the previous year, just after the March action.' What was more significant, the Communists had grown at the expense of the Social Democrats (SPD), who suffered losses despite their unification with the remnants of the former USPD. This must be regarded as the greatest achievement, since winning *organised* workers was, according to Lenin, the main Communist task. Also significant was the prevalence of men over women (191,845 to 26,710) owing to their role in industrial and public life, as well as gains in trade unions and county councils – an absolute majority in 80 town councils, a relative majority in 170 others, over 6,000 Communist councillors, nearly 1,000 organised groups within the trade unions with 400 Communists in top positions. The Communists were strongest in numbers and influence in the main areas like Berlin, Hamburg, and Rheinland.

The annual report of the Leipzig Party Congress gives a dazzling picture of Communist activity of 1922: creation of special sections in municipalities and co-operatives; women's, youth, and children's sections; work among farmers and farmhands; legal advice and assistance for political prisoners and their families. Besides a Communist press agency and 34 dailies, they possessed seven periodicals including *The International, The Communist Trade Unionist* and *The Communist Farm Labourer.*

The Party also succeeded in creating a 'Red Relief Association' which helped the thousands of victims of the March Action with some 8.5 million marks. An 'Aid for Russia' section gained donations from many parts of Germany. Collections effected by children and adolescents alone amounted to 8 million marks.

Party schools were created in several parts of the country and special teachers circulated from district to district spreading theoretical Communist knowledge. Publications of Russian literature, old and new, and imports of Russian films were means of stimulating understanding and sympathy for the Soviet Union as well as the Communist Party.

All this invaluable information is supplied by Ruth Fischer, whose hostility to Ernst survived his death by some eighteen years. Of course, it does not occur to her to give any credit or so much as connect the gains with Ernst's term in office.

After the March upheaval when Levi, Reuter, and other able men from the former USPD, with independent minds and revolutionary experience, deserted the Party, there remained no-one to contest Ernst's supremacy. Brandler, the only man to achieve repute, was in Moscow and had no influence in German affairs. Thal-

heimer, the erudite marxist and keen revolutionary, was never a de-
signer of current policy. Paul Froelich, the pamphleteer and propagandist, confessed to me in a private talk that, left to himself, he
was never able to find an answer to an unforeseen problem. Klara
Zetkin was in Russia most of the time on account of ill health. The
other old Spartacists, Pieck, Eberlein, Heckert, all gifted, devoted
Communists, were good administrators – 'a brilliant supporting
cast, no more'.

Under Ernst Meyer's leadership the Party became a force
to reckon with in 1923, and was in a position to make a serious bid
for power. Yet despite his prominent position he tended to minimise his own merits: 'A child could now lead the Party. It is all
there, all worked out. We only have to follow Lenin's guidance.'

During his entire term of office Ernst faced not only fierce
animosity from the Left – Ruth Fischer and Maslow – who regarded any constructive Party activities as 'Communist reformism'
and retreat from revolution, but also, for some obscure reason, opposition from Radek, and particularly from August Guralsky, who
lived in Berlin and played an important part in German affairs. Although there never was a basic disagreement on current policy between Ernst and these two men, a subterranean campaign of vilification was always in progress.

Life was taking a more or less normal course, and Ernst was
working without a break. In 1922 I went to Heidelberg for three
months and his letters give further proof of his difficulties:

16 May 1922, Berlin

... Session after session before the opening of the Central
Committee and working out of the resolutions, and preparation for my own speech. On Sunday my speech, which I
had to combine with Radek's who was refused permission
to appear. I spoke tolerably. Then discussion, a closing
speech and a resolution committee in the evening. On Monday chairmanship of the Central Committee, Senior Coun-

cil, order procedure, debates in parliament, and again chairmanship of the Central Committee session; *three* articles on the Central Committee until midnight, and then reading Paul's pamphlet until two in the morning.

Today party meeting over our tactics (warding off accusations of my 'reformism'), a long speech in the Diet on the extradition of Italians, and correcting proofs. Now at last I can get around to writing to you.

20 May 1922

My holiday will start soon after the 28th of May. Unfortunately I cannot come sooner: tomorrow Magdeburg, Monday parliamentary conferences, Tuesday Commission (Neunerkommission) for the International Workers' Congress, Wednesday Central Committee session, Thursday secretary-conference, Sunday Berlin Area Conference. And every day Parliament: 'Genua', 'Aid for Russia', etc.

I am attending the full parliamentary sessions at the moment, and have to watch out in case President Leinert plays any of his dirty tricks.

I didn't get home until very late last night and am really tired and nervous. I have to go to Magdeburg at 10 o'clock this evening, and on Monday morning to the continuation of the law debate, where my presence is absolutely necessary. I also have to write an article today – and, as yet, have no time to rest or read.

. . . Yesterday I had my first clash with Maslow . . . and today he has been taking me to task over another matter in the *Rote Fahne*. But I am confident that in a few weeks the difficulties will be overcome. I am truly longing to hear nothing of Party policy.

It was tolerable in normal times, and Ernst managed to deal with the conflicts in his quiet way. But in the summer of 1922 Germany was shaken by a new crisis. On 24 June, the Foreign Minister, Walter Rathenau, one of the finest heads of the democratic forces in the Weimar Republic, was murdered by right-wing extremists. The workers were enraged and called for action. It was the moment for the Party to offer common action on a basis comprehensible and acceptable to the politically-minded workers, which is the essence of United Front tactics. The trade unions were not at all keen to enter such an uneasy alliance. But here was a case where Communists could not be ignored nor their collaboration wantonly rejected.

Still, there was much disruption in the new SPD-KPD United Front, and the Social Democrats were aided in this by a large number of Communists. Not only was the Communist Workers' Party (KAPD) against any compromise, but the former USPD and SPD workers, who only recently joined the Communists, were characteristically reluctant to mix with yesterday's associates. Their genuine hatred and disappointment was mixed with a desire to prove themselves worthy of their new beliefs, and they demanded 'action – not talk'.

Even members of the Central Committee, reflecting the mood of large sections of the Party, fought tooth and nail against any deals with the SPD and the trade unions. Ernst wrote to me on 5 July 1922:

Ruth Fischer is determined, full of rage and eagerly looking forward to settling old scores. The trade unions fear us and therefore do not mention any breach in their letter. We answered with an ultimatum – of *political* demands: withdrawal of the SPD from the Government; dissolution of the Reichstag; new elections or general strike.

But we do not want a breach on purely formal grounds (for instance, over their criticism that we broke confidentiality in the course of the negotiations).

Some idiots on the Central Committee are bent on a breach over rather formal issues. An incorrect resolution was passed advocating an abrupt breach – and then I, diplomat that I am, took over the job of formulating the written version of this resolution, phoned for support (some members were absent) and reversed the decision.

More surprising was the sceptical attitude of the 'guests', the Russian emissaries, since the Bolshevik Party had been imbued with the theory and practice of compromises and united actions with Russian equivalents of the SPD – up to its victory. But the 'guests' were impatient. They wanted action at all costs. They had learned nothing from the debacle of the March Action. And the submissiveness to the great architects of the Russian Revolution knew no limits. An excruciating example of it is contained in the following letter from Ernst:

> 24 July 1922, 7.30 a.m.
>
> . . . The last two days upset me so much that I could not sleep. Until Saturday afternoon everything went smoothly. Then Kaethe's husband [Guralsky – RLM] arrived, set up a small faction and proceeded to threaten us at the evening session with a crisis in the Party unless the Central Committee withdrew its resolution in favour of his views. His entire speech was an act of political blackmail of the worst kind. To increase the pressure he quite explicitly aligned himself with Maslow's Left. I was utterly enraged and demanded that he speaks just as openly at the Central Assembly. If it was true that the Party was in danger, it was his duty to make his warning in public; otherwise he was committing a crime against the Party.
>
> This open declaration of war and my demand that he should bring his blackmail out into the open startled him and shook his self-confidence. But the Central Committee, with the exception of Walcher and Hecket, capitulated and swallowed the essentials of Guralsky's resolution.
>
> I arrived home at midnight and was, of course, compelled to alter my speech, which I then delivered badly and listlessly at the Central Assembly (bound as I was by the new resolution of the Central Committee, although I had nothing to blame myself for).
>
> Then Kaethe's husband spoke. His delivery was even worse than

Ernst Meyer
in his student days

Heinrich
Brandler

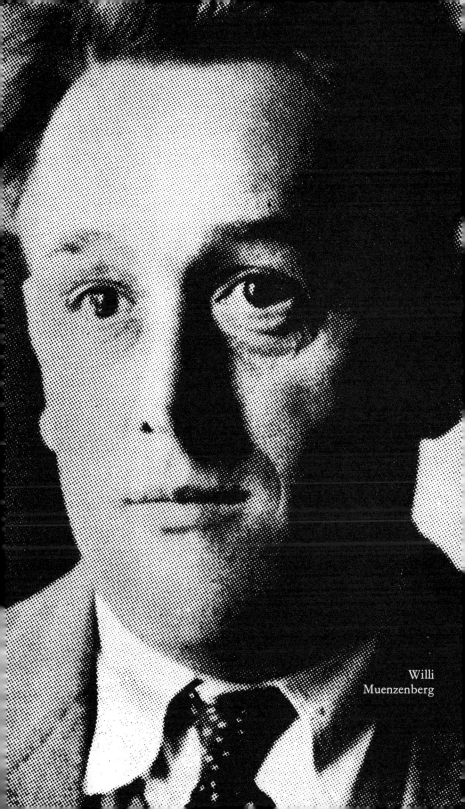

Willi
Muenzenberg

Ruth Fischer

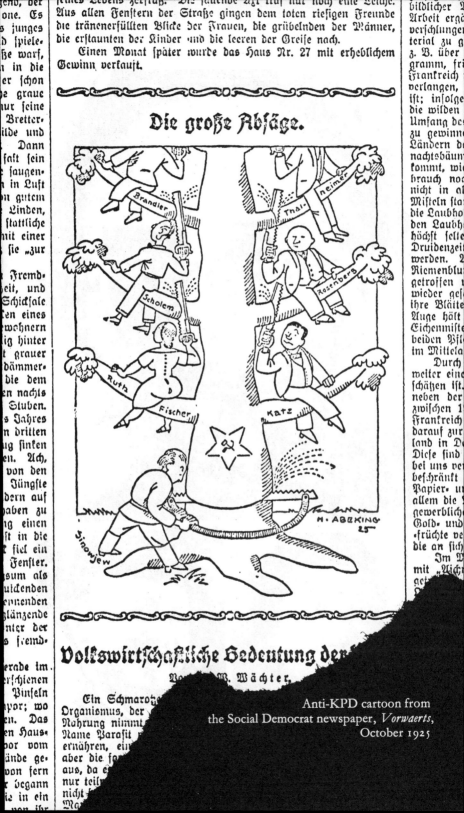

Aus allen Fenstern der Straße gingen dem toten riesigen Freunde die tränenerfüllten Blicke der Frauen, die grübelnden der Männer, die erstaunten der Kinder und die leeren der Greise nach.

Einen Monat später wurde das Haus Nr. 27 mit erheblichem Gewinn verkauft.

Die große Absäge.

Volkswirtschaftliche Bedeutung der

Von W. Wächter.

Ein Schmarotzer
Organismus, der
Nahrung nimmt
ernähren, ein
aber die
aus, da
nur teil
nicht

Anti-KPD cartoon from the Social Democrat newspaper, *Vorwaerts*, October 1925

Karl Radek

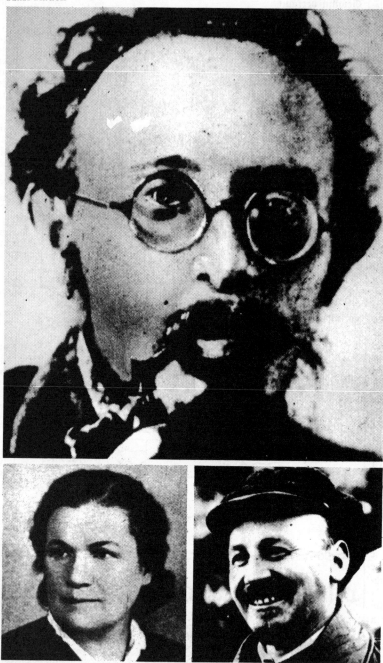

Anna Pankratova   Nikolai Bukharin

Grigori Zinoviev

Arkadi Maslow

Paul Levi

Richard Sorge

Ernst Meyer at 33,
Moscow 1920

Werktätige Frauen

Kämpft mit uns!

Wählt

LISTE 4

KOMMUNISTEN

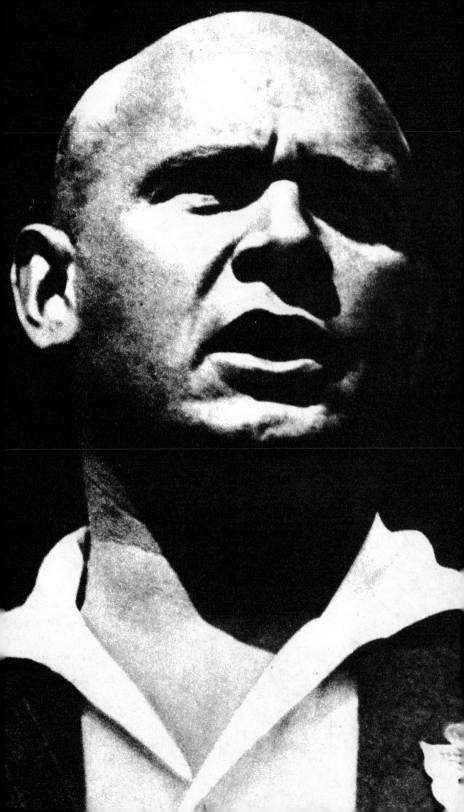

Opposite, Ernst Thaelmann:
Thaelmann, at left below, marching with RFB
(Red Front Fighters League)

Thaelmann speaking at Red Front rally, 1926

Berlin police in action
against demonstrating
workers
May Day, 1929

Ernst Meyer and Rosa Leviné-Meyer
with her son Eugen, 1925

mine and the substance of his speech was nonsense. The discussion, as was to be expected, ended in an almost unanimous rejection of Guralsky's views. The Central Committee was held solely to blame and its representatives now all spoke against their previous resolution under the pressure of the Central Assembly, with the exception of Boettcher! Pieck made it worse by his clumsy declaration that, in order to avoid a crisis, the Central Committee had admitted mistakes which it never committed.

In my closing speech I made a vigorous attack on the critics. I was so upset that I stamped with a chair at an interruption by Guralsky and dealt with them so severely that Pieck sent me a note saying 'moderate a little', and the critics broke into loud heckling once or twice. The result: a pitiful defeat of Guralsky and Maslow; Maslow was left with a minority of five. Ten more sympathised with him, or rather with Guralsky, but voted for the concluding resolution of the Central Committee. I too voted for it though it contained much rubbish, though harmless.

The best and largest organisations: Rhineland, Middle Germany, Saxony, Wuertemberg, and so on, supported me.

My opponents' rage knows no bounds. I know that they will leave *no stone* unturned. But I am almost pleased at the idea of fighting this struggle. I shall have to spend at least three days weekly in the provinces. It means much travel and much work. But it is vital that we bring about the health and stabilisation of the Party once and for all.

I regret the fact that Guralsky made himself so impossible. The final incentive was a foolish letter from Zinoviev who by the way is isolated in the Executive. He suggests actions of our own, at least a 24 hour protest strike! (Everything about Zinoviev is of course confidential!).

The forces at play and the mood during the Rathenau crisis can be understood from Ernst's letters to me at the time:

Morale of the country excellent. Zwikow in the hands of the workers. Spontaneous eruptions everywhere.

Attempts of the SPD to isolate us – repulsed. Despite our sharp public criticism new negotiations with all organisations tomorrow!

They both need and fear us. The USPD is in a critical position. They wanted to enter the Cabinet but the bourgeoisie won't accept them. The question of the dissolution of the Reichstag is acute once again . . .

30 June, 1922

. . . We mustered an evening edition of 80,000, and a morning edition of 120,000 copies. Hurrah !

The situation is marvellous for us: two agreements and on Tuesday a common demonstration, but with freedom of criticism of the SPD and USPD. The trade unions have great respect for us.

Morale of the Central Committee and the *Rote Fahne* – good. Though the SPD will betray, the workers will be on *our* side. The USPD plays a pitiful role.

July, 1922

Tomorrow morning the re-appearance of the *Rote Fahne*. It was high time. We were already lagging behind as *Vorwaerts* has been published as an 'Information Sheet'.

. . . The session ended in a real fight. Bundles of documents were flying like rockets at the Heidelberg Castle illumination. A USPD man threw his own USPD colleague like a missile against the conservatives and our people were hopping on to the rostrum like sparrows.

Two days later came the climax:

Sunday morning, 9 July

. . . I am desperate that I can't be with you. I could almost cry. I already had a sleeping car ticket. I meant to stay with you all Monday though Pieck said it would raise a storm in the

Central Committee. But even the hope and joy of spending
Sunday with you was fading hour by hour.
Yesterday *Vorwaerts* announced their breach with us. That required
a new session, a proclamation and an article. Jacob
(Walcher) had not finished his part in time. The second
session started at 8, ended about 9.30 ? but I had to go again,
as on every evening, to our editor's office and could not
leave before 12.30. I sank to bed very sad and exhausted.

The announced breach caused no alarm. And the
atmosphere in which the policy was carried out makes it even more
commendable. My letters to Ernst confirm it:

July, 1922

You asked for reports on the mood of the Party. It is not so good.
Workers in one of the best plants, who unanimously voted
for the Communists, could not be persuaded to join the
demonstration: Nothing will come of it anyhow, better
work and earn some money.
. . . The Central Committee has no proper policy. *The Communist
workers did not wish to collaborate with the SPD.* But a
split now would cause a lot of bad feeling. I also think, personally, that we should try and keep up a united front, at
least for a while yet . . . one should not let them shake us
off. Of course, criticism could not be dispensed with. But
you, the diplomat, will know best how to prevent an undesirable breach.

Indeed, at a private session of the Leipzig Congress in January 1923, Ernst was to declare:
. . . it did not prevent me from using my influence outside official
sessions to avoid a breach and to insure a policy profitable
to our Party. I was well aware of the mood in our districts
and boroughs and did not need telegrams and letters from
district officers and secretaries to tell me. I knew that the
German workers, that our own supporters, would not understand if we broke off negotiations on trifling matters. I

struggled against the Berliners who tried with all their might to impose contrary views on the Central Committee, as well as against the heavy pressure exercised by Kleine.

I further reported to him:

. . . Schlesinger and Lotte Kornfeld attack you vigorously. My judgement was only a general one – I have no real opinion because I have not studied matters sufficiently.

R.Fischer attacked the Central Committee – they *unanimously* accepted a very sharp resolution against you, *against the United Front*. This surprises me a great deal as Boehning expressed himself quite differently. Their strategy: the Central Committee must go and Maslow and Ruth Fischer must replace it.

The withdrawal of the SPD (the breach) only proved that the Communists had not 'lost face' in the process of negotiations. And it was undoubtedly more favourable to let the Social Democrats take upon themselves the odium of being 'splitters'. There were, however, points when Ernst himself advocated breach and his tone was so pungent that the Central Committee decided to exclude him from the negotiations. He was only asked to take the floor when the situation demanded particular boldness. Yet on other occasions he was accused of going too far in his concessions:

July 1922

How they instigate feeling against me I learned yesterday again. Eberlein sent me a copy of Maslow's letter to Radek which reads:

'On the first day of the Rathenau campaign everything was going well. Then Ernst Meyer appeared on Sunday and promptly succumbed to the Trade Union bosses.'

'The result of my negotiations', Ernst later reminded the delegates at the private session of the Leipzig Congress, 'was that other members of the Central Committee stated that I was too harsh with the representatives of the SPD and the ADGB [National Trade Union Federation] and that this method of dealing with other workers' organisations was not permissible: it was decided that it would perhaps be better to let other comrades speak, as I was too severe. Indeed, I was only asked to take part in the common session when it was necessary to put our view very strongly even at the risk of a breach.

'. . . Comrades, this is the "acquiescence" in my negotiations with the SPD and ADGB. This is my "succumbing to the United Front rubbish" which Maslow spoke of in his letter to Radek.'

They all tried to place responsibility on his shoulders for the disappointing end. Ernst thought the attacks particularly treacherous, and I have never seen him so upset. I remember that our visiting Russian friends often voiced their astonishment, in private conversations of course, that he did so little to combat the Left: 'They are flourishing on accusations and demagogy and have become a power in Berlin. You are too fair. You must meet them on their own terms.'

Which meant fighting with their foul methods, and this was not Ernst's strength. He fought them in his way and apparently quite mercilessly. Not for nothing was he their main target, not Brandler nor anyone else. But he fought with political arguments in the best tradition of democratic procedure which alone, in the long run, safeguards the functioning of a sane Party.

There is no doubt that it was the Rathenau affair which brought about Ernst's downfall. The vigour of the Left's propaganda, their unscrupulous fighting method; Zinoviev's over-estimating the revolutionary potential of the event and blaming the Party for not going far enough; the submissiveness of the majority of leaders, alive to any command or *hint* of the Comintern as was expressed in the incident with Guralsky – all helped to create the appropriate conditions. And, of course, Ernst's own helplessness in coping with what he considered 'personal' matters must be regarded as a considerable contribution to his fall.

The invalidity of the attacks on him can best be gauged from the testimony of Klara Zetkin who said that all the isolated mistakes could not erase the fact that the Rathenau campaign was the *first* large-scale unified, resolutely carried out action of the Communist Party.

Ernst's most hostile rival, Brandler, was no less outspoken, asserting that the German Communist Party rarely, if ever, carried out an action so well, with such clarity and resolution.

In his book on October 1923 which was to serve as an apology for Brandler, Thalheimer quoted Zinoviev as saying there was not the slightest doubt that on the whole the KPD applied United Front tactics with great success and succeeded in winning over the majority of the German workers – a thing one could not even dream of two to three years before.

Thalheimer only forgot to add that it was not Brandler's but Ernst's doing. Brandler took over from Ernst a strong consolidated Party and brought it to disaster within nine months of his rule – from January to October, 1923.

4.

Moscow, 1922

In August 1922, Ernst was summoned to Moscow where the first spectacular post-Revolution trial was taking place. The defendants, a number of leading personalities from the Social Revolutionary Party, were accused of collaborating with foreign interventionist forces in their attempt to crush the Bolsheviks. Their guilt needed little confirmation and was not based on 'confessions'; their activities were known throughout the world.

The defendants made no bones about their relentless hatred towards the Bolsheviks. They belonged to a party with a brilliant record of fighting Tsarism, and they now behaved in the best tradition of their heroic past. But the harm they caused by aiding the intervention and by their terrorist activities – through which Lenin himself nearly fell victim – were too fresh in the memory, and the workers demanded retribution. Death sentences were pronounced and met with no great criticism even abroad.

Yet the Soviet government was reluctant to carry out the sentences. The civil war was over, the defendants presented no great danger to the more or less stabilised state. Concerned with the impression the executions would make on workers abroad, the government sought opinions from Communist leaders of other countries. Together with Klara Zetkin, Ernst Meyer was to represent the German party. But the decision had been reached before his arrival. Trotsky demanded that the sentences be postponed, the condemned kept as hostages and executed in case of any further terrorist activities by their party. This was opposed by Ernst: 'A complete acquittal seemed to me to be politically more intelligent, but only Klara [Zetkin] and the French supported me.'

Ernst was cautious in his letters but told me how upset and worried he was about the decision. He had a private encounter with Trotsky who tried to win him over to his notion and who was not himself, of course, a man to be persuaded.

Yet this was a time when the powerful Russian Party could still be overruled. Ernst's opinion triumphed:

7 August

This evening the Russian Central Committee dropped the superfluous hostage stuff against which I (alone with Klara) was fighting yesterday. My joy helped me overcome my stomach trouble which had bothered me all day long. I am very happy about the decision and am therefore thinking joyfully of you.

Ernst's letters also conveyed the pupil, ready to learn and admire though never shutting his eyes to weaknesses:

I generally dislike the tone at the Comintern: a mixture of German brutality and Russian spontaneity . . . The new course [NEP] produces a certain reckless egotism instead of the former boundless altruism. The 'top' also grow more West-European, they are more diplomatic and more efficient . . . On the whole the new course stimulates everything: more people, more work, more goods, more trade and initiative, more confidence . . . I am not a dreamer, but everything is so exciting and refreshing. There is liveliness and greatness even in making mistakes . . . I should like to write a few articles right away. But I shall do it in Berlin. You must remind me and then correct them.

That same autumn, we travelled together to Russia. As a

member of the Executive of the Comintern Ernst was obliged to take part periodically in its activities – some three months at a time.

Moscow! I was treading on holy ground. Oh, I knew it, the whole town, the Kremlin, the churches, but now the high walls of the Kremlin and its huge halls were magically opened to me, the Jewish girl to whom entry to the city had once been barred. The Bolshoi, to which Ernst as well as other top leaders had permanent access, with a seat in the imperial box, was also opened to me. In a similar theatre in St Petersburg Anna Karenina, my heroine, was humiliated by arrogant, shallow aristocrats.

On the first day of our arrival we ran into Karl Radek, to whose stories I listened with the delight of a sentimental mother to the prattle of her baby – my heart was swelling. Radek solemnly congratulated me on my marriage: 'Of course, your association was no secret to me, but to mention it before would have been an indiscretion; now it is an obligation.' He turned to his usual buffoonery: 'We are going to pass a resolution for your husband to get the right girl secretary to teach him Russian.'

I parried: 'You had plenty of them and your Russian is still inadequate.'

'Oh, but it is not the tongue with which I talk to them.'

This gay cordiality seemed to me a token of the new brotherhood of socialist society. It was, in fact, almost the last friendly meeting between Radek and Meyer.

The town was buzzing with tales of luxury and opulence in the lives of Comintern leaders. In fact, we were only allotted one room with a tiny hall and adjoining washing area, which was the best of the lot, Ernst being chairman of the German Politbureau. The hotel was infested with mice and rats running through the long corridors and rooms. Food was plentiful, but stale and rotten. Out of the four eggs we received for breakfast at least three were unfit for consumption.

I was resolved to accept the difficulties, food and all, as my share of the suffering endured by the land of my choice. But after a few days of gallant striving I was laid up with a high fever and badly upset stomach. One of my bourgeois visitors saw the food we ate, insisted we never touch it again, and provided cooked meals for the duration of our stay.

The Bolsheviks were trying hard to live up to their socialist ideas. Living standards in our circle were as a rule far below those of my non-Communist friends, since Communists received less pay than their bourgeois equivalents – a so-called 'Party maximum' which hardly exceeded the wages of a highly qualified factory worker. This spartan self-restraint did not last very long. But even while it lasted, it was slightly illusory like most self-imposed 'idealistic'restrictions. Lebedev, who watched every penny in Berlin and ordered the cheapest dishes in restaurants, was better supplied than his 'Party maximum' allowed. The extras were disguised as presents. The title of 'Bolshevik' was second to none, equal now to that of aristocracy. No wage restrictions could eliminate that discrepancy.

A great friendship developed between me and Lebedev's wife. She was brought up by her grandmother, lived in better conditions and received a much better education than her husband. It did not prevent her from cheerfully accepting the lot of the wife of a Russian textile worker and the constant anguish which went with his political activities. Hard work, privation, discomfort, did not seem to make any difference to those people. On my last two journeys to Russia in 1931 and 1932 when famine crippled the country, I often thought that this almost uncanny vitality was one of their greatest revolutionary assets. German workers simply could not survive under such conditions, let alone do eight hours work.

The Party did not seem to have changed much at the top. Zinoviev, whom I met in his Kremlin quarters for a modest tea, was the same unassuming, cordial comrade as he had been in a second-rate hotel in Berlin. Bukharin was still indulging in jokes and pranks. The general mood defied the established pattern of revolutionary climax followed by political apathy and tiredness. The Revolution unleashed unheard of energies; initiative and experiment were awakened and encouraged. The Party and the state apparatus were revived by gifted energetic men and women, drawn from the working population for administration and government work. The Revolution had not stopped, it demanded new tasks and its leaders were spending themselves by the inhuman effort they had to make.

It is also true that the new tasks made the Russian leaders gradually unfit to direct the revolutionary movement abroad. They were speedily unlearning the art of revolutionary strategy and tactics, and their interference abroad proved fatal.

This was also the time of the first purges; an attempt to rid the Party of alien elements, but had nothing in common with Stalin's purges of the late thirties. Loss of the Party-book did not even lead automatically to the loss of position. Yet the purges caused great distress and even occasional suicides. The first result was panic and a sense of insecurity, making some of the best Party members resort to lies and deception. Proletarian origin being the number one qualification for Party membership, Anna Pankratova, one of the finest and most devoted revolutionaries of her generation, concealed her 'middle-class peasant' origin from the Party.

Fear and submissiveness were growing around me, and I came to witness them in a most depressing way. People began to admit fear of the notorious 'knock on the door', which always occurred at night to add a sense of shock.

'Why don't you complain? You speak so nicely of "our Soviet". You could at least try to modify the unwarranted cruelty of the timing.'

'We cannot interfere in administrative matters. What do you think? It could be taken for anti-Bolshevism . . .'

How refreshing a solitary case of defiance was! I was once taken on a tour of the Kremlin by a member of its former staff. There were many objects named 'red' – red balcony, red chamber, red gates. I ventured a remark; 'Red, red – and how much red blood was shed?'

'And is being spilt now', said our guide with great dignity. His views and animosity were no secret to the new masters but it did not occur to them to dismiss the man on account of his feelings or *private* remarks which could do no harm.

A visit to the Museum of the Revolution gave me an idea of what those callous GPU-men had had to suffer at the hands of their adversaries, often kind, cultured people. Crammed with age-old devices of torture and some 'contemporary' ones, you shuddered at the sight of lampshades, gloves and other 'utilities' constructed of human skin torn from living bodies. The GPU-men were too hardened to think of people's feelings and of sparing them. It was too early to forgive.

A hopeful contrast to this seemed the behaviour of the militia-men. We could watch them pleading with petty offenders – to obey the law, whereas 'laying hands' on them seemed out of the question. The Red soldiers too, in their newly created club, were more like students, eager to ask questions and tell us interesting stories.

It seemed to me a country unmatched in strength and endurance. Life was still hard enough but living standards were improving. 'More than yesterday' determined the general mood and created an atmosphere of exhilarating confidence. I never saw an empty seat at a meeting or a theatre, nor such enthusiastic audiences. One day Trotsky was to speak at a Party meeting in the Hall of Columns, and all Moscow was on its feet. Everybody knew where the hundreds of excited people were hurriedly streaming, exchanging nods and smiles.

Under the surface a fight against Trotsky was already in progress. Strangely enough, the little taunts which started it, like the occasional omitting of his name, putting it on the wrong side of a list or other seemingly insignificant trifles were quickly noticed and debated by ordinary Muscovites. They proved more sensitive than the Party, which was almost unaware of it. But it did not matter one way or the other: friend or foe, no one wanted to forgo the treat of hearing Trotsky speak. Hundreds of people packed the huge hall long before the meeting started, more had to be turned away. When we arrived, large crowds were still gathered outside the building hoping against hope for a seat. As Ernst's private interpreter I had my seat beside him on the platform.

Trotsky's power as an orator had become legendary. I heard

him for the first time and was seized by the same exaltation which completely captivated his other listeners. Besides, I had a private reason for excitement – Trotsky was speaking on foreign affairs and his criticism of the March Action confirmed my own views. The magic of his unique voice and the brilliance of the delivery were intoxicating and at moments seemed even to outweigh the content of his words. It was impossible to keep a clear mind.

Even more than the stormy ovations, the unwillingness to disperse afterwards showed Trotsky's effect on his audience. They all rose to their feet but seemed to be held back by an almost physical fusion with the speaker. I thought I understood how this man could achieve the impossible, create an army out of nothing, make it fight and conquer. No one could resist him. But it would be a half-truth to leave it at that, for suddenly everything changed. A different Trotsky made his appearance – Trotsky the man, self-centred and vain.

Ernst had advised me to send copies of Leviné's biography to Lenin and Trotsky, and to the head of the Comintern, Zinoviev. The cover showed an Expressionist picture of Leviné which grossly distorted his real personality. When I was introduced to Trotsky, I was naturally keen to establish that the painting did not do Leviné justice. Trotsky objected and went into an elaborate appreciation of modern art. Amidst people still fanatically hanging on his lips, the topic was not only out of place, it was also out of context. He was talking in the same authoritative manner as before, indifferent to whether I could follow or wished to take an interest in this new subject, oblivious to the atmosphere charged with the impact of his speech, to everything, obviously following an urge to impress on a completely different subject.

I listened in bewildered silence. Ernst was surprised but proud of the attention paid to me, but I was not even flattered, feeling I had witnessed Trotsky split into two different people.

The revolutionary celebrations, like the Revolution itself, began in Leningrad. A huge parade and procession with banners and flowers marching to the place where the martyrs of the Revolution were buried, initiated the event. Pouring rain, which never seemed to stop, was no deterrent to the festive mood.

Zinoviev dominated the city. The crowds hung on his words, responded cheerfully to his little jokes, his 'down with the counter-revolutionary rain!' went from mouth to mouth, from column to column. His popularity was enormous and he prided himself on his capacity to perceive the mood and aspirations of the masses by keeping his ear to the ground.

Poverty and bad weather were powerless against so much enthusiasm and determination. The foreign guests were rushed from one school to another, from one club to the other, and judging by the beaming faces of children their appearance and short speeches made up for all the hard work of painting, decorating, performing and even for the not-too-richly laid tables.

Theatres, concert halls were filled with people who had never dreamed of going near them. New companies, new experiments were mushrooming, and dedicated, selfless servants of art did everything to maintain the old high standards. I sometimes asked myself how and why they managed to keep the Bolshoi. It was in such contrast to the times, to the people, to the *women* who looked almost sexless now in their drab, deforming clothes. What must their men feel after witnessing feminine beauty elevated to such heights?

My Russian friends were appalled: 'Destroy beauty, withhold it from the workers? They created it, the leisure, for others to indulge in art and beauty.'

The Moscow celebrations were also carried out with great pomp and enthusiasm, and the star was Trotsky. His speech, at least his voice and manner, captivated even the diplomatic corps and the foreign press. His words seemed to hit the opposite buildings on the immense Red Square and resound in a clear echo. It produced an uncanny impression, as if there were two Trotskys present. Even his adversaries paid him tribute by admiring glances and astonished head shaking. It happened once or twice that a parading column failed to notice his presence. But then somebody apparently told them and they stopped, all heads turned in his direction, and the whisper 'Trotsky, Trotsky' went from mouth to mouth. He, the War Commissar, was taking the parade in a military fashion, his hand at his cap, during some six hours on the cold Russian November day. I left the tribunal about 4 o'clock, frozen to the bone, Ernst was shivering and intended to follow me soon, but I waited in vain for another two hours: 'I could not tear myself away from that man – how did he do it ? I felt small beside him and would have felt cowardly to leave as long as he was there.'

The Moscow festivities were normally opened by Lenin at a special session of the Central Soviet at the Bolshoi Theatre. Would he appear this time ? The question was eagerly discussed by everybody, including bitter enemies of the state. Even they showed a genuine concern about Lenin's health: let's have Lenin, if we must accept the lot . . . This time he could not make it. He struggled in vain, and the sad announcement of his absence was made at the very last moment. But we did not know how serious his condition was when, at the same time, it was announced that he would definitely take his place at the Comintern Congress.

The Congress was held in the former throne-hall of the Kremlin. Gold, ivory, semi-precious stones formed the background to the rough wooden benches installed for the delegates. The throne, carefully covered, was tucked away in a corner of the small platform which had been erected. And all the pomp and splendour also seemed hidden away – the crowd that now ruled the place hardly noticed it. Lenin entered the room and hurriedly moved towards the platform. Terribly excited, he kept mopping his face with a white handkerchief. All got up to greet him and clapped, but there were none of the usual ovations since Lenin's aversion to any form of ostentation was well known. But the restraint was also an instinctive response to a strange almost tangible quietude emanating from him, numbing us into silence.

In an unconventional plain manner Lenin started his speech. There were endless speculations about who was the better of the two great orators, Lenin or Trotsky. Lenin undoubtedly tipped the scales. It was his sincerity, the feeling he conveyed that he put the last vestige of his being into *what* he wished to say, which made his speech so unique.

The official language of the Comintern was German. Lenin mastered it almost to perfection, but a group of the best-known interpreters was placed at his disposal to meet any emergency. When he stumbled over a word he said it in Russian and waited with his hand at his ear for the translation. The answer came from everywhere, but he shook his head, sometimes two, three, or more times until accepting the right word. He then made a gesture as if picking it up with his hand. The man famous for his cool detachment and sober, incisive brain was at the same time deeply moving. I could never remain unmoved when I spoke of or remembered that experience. I considered it the greatest event of my life. It was Lenin's last speech to the Comintern.

It is fair to add that not everybody shared my feeling. Ruth Fischer who was sitting beside me shrugged her shoulders and exclaimed: 'There is nothing one can do with this speech.'

Trotsky spoke afterwards. I was too overwhelmed to listen and understand. I could only watch. No two other great men could be more different from each other than Lenin and Trotsky. It seemed that Trotsky was more in his element among huge masses where the power of his voice overwhelmed and magnetized everybody. Here he decided to translate his own speech to the Russian and then to the French delegates. This struck me as unnecessary bravado and vanity, yet I must add that many of the delegates were enthusiastic about such a tour de force.

5.

Ernst Meyer's Fall from Power, 1922

In November 1922, Ernst left Berlin in high spirits to attend the Fourth Comintern Congress in Moscow. The German party, of which Paul Levi had almost despaired, was functioning well. The workers' confidence was restored, the misunderstanding with the Comintern cleared up in a 'frank, cordial talk' with its head, Zinoviev. The Party was also growing steadily in influence, and Ernst was particularly proud of his ability to apply intricate United Front tactics with a minimum of error.

Yet soon after his arrival in Moscow Ernst's fortunes began to change. Radek's cordiality towards him soon turned to petty hostility. It had nothing to do with political controversy, at least as far as the methods of Radek's campaign were concerned. The reasons seemed strictly personal and aimed first of all at discrediting Ernst in the eyes of the German delegates assembled in Moscow for the Congress. Radek would receive Ernst at official sessions with: 'Was it ballet or opera last night?' Or: 'We all know where to look for Ernst Meyer when we need him, at a show with his young wife.' At that time rejection of 'bourgeois culture' was nearly a revolutionary duty, with the classical ballet of the Bolshoi a particularly favourite target for sneers, and Radek exploited that mood. Although his insinuations could not be taken seriously, they signalled that Ernst was falling out of favour, and quite a number of the German delegates were ready to go along with the idea.

There was, however, a serious motive for Radek's behaviour, and Ruth Fischer provides a clue: 'After Levi's exit Radek praised Thalheimer and Brandler as genuine examples of the revolutionary spirit . . . Brandler had a much firmer hand than the refined intellectual Ernst Meyer.'

It was also true that a serious political controversy had broken out between Ernst and Zinoviev over the term 'Workers' Government', which the latter insisted was a synonym for the Dictatorship of the Proletariat – an interpretation Ernst Meyer challenged. In Saxony-Thuringia the SPD had achieved a parliamentary majority and built an exclusively Labour government. They were prepared to grant the Communists proportional representation – four seats in all. Should the Party accept the offer? The Congress decided in the affirmative. It was a dangerous step in contradiction to the Communist doctrine against entering, as a minority, any coalition government. In an article of December 1922, 'The Results of the Fourth Comintern Congress', Ernst summarised his views: 'The character of a workers' government is not determined by its personnel but by the policy which it carries out.

'Liberal labour governments which might be formed in England, or the social-democratic labour governments which have arisen in certain German free states, although contributing to the disintegration of capitalism, can in no way be confused with real Workers' governments, which seriously attempt to take up the struggle against the bourgeoisie. The Communists can, therefore, only join a Labour government and share in its responsibilities under the condition that it has the direct support of working-class organisations (factory councils) and if the government actually adopts real measures against the bourgeoisie. When such a government comes into being with Communist support, it will still not be identical with the Dictatorship of the Proletariat, but can act as its starting point through the struggles which will necessarily take place between the working class and the bourgeoisie.'

It was obvious from the start that the entire German bourgeoisie would regard the entrance of the Communists into the government as a serious challenge not confined to an isolated locality but to Germany as a whole. The central powers were not expected to recognise the legality of the Workers' government, and armed intervention was regarded as unavoidable.

The exceptional conditions of inflation-stricken Germany seemed to justify the change of tactics. The country was shifting to the left because of a calamity which was daily changing the pattern of life and uprooting age-old traditions. Therefore, it was possible to assume that an attempt to remove forcibly a parliamentary elected government would be met with armed resistance by the workers and in the process lead to the revolutionary climax – Dictatorship of the Proletariat.

Ernst vigorously objected to Zinoviev's 'synonym' and events proved soon enough that it was an adventurous illusion to present the Workers' government as another form of the Dictatorship. In the end Ernst's view was accepted, but Zinoviev, no longer used to being opposed, was very irritated by his intervention. And what could be easier than to insinuate that 'Meyer underestimated the revolutionary strength of the workers' – a favourite common denominator for opportunism and Right deviation.

Ernst was a little baffled at the hostility of Radek and Zinoviev but saw no threat to his position in the Party. And now he was given a good chance to clear up a very important matter, the validity of the Left's attacks on him. Lenin wanted to go into the controversy and to acquaint himself with the essence of the Left's arguments, so he invited the two chief protagonists – Ernst and Ruth Fischer. The main object of the attacks by the Left was Ernst's conduct of the Rathenau campaign. I had no doubt that Lenin would give Ernst his full support. Yet, tired and sad, he returned from the battlefield; Lenin, he told me, could see no fundamental cause for dissent and no unbridgeable obstacles to a fruitful collaboration.

Ernst's fate as leader of the Party was decided in Moscow. Besides intrigue, misguided ideas, and the personal ambitions of others, a genuine sentiment stood behind the decision. The Russians could not imagine this quiet, to all appearances cold, retiring man fighting a revolutionary battle. They did not trust him. They confused his unbending, wholesome dignity with arrogance and lack of flexibility. It seemed to be a clash of two different cultures. Even Lenin's definition of the German Communist Party, which had lost at least 10,000 lives during the short revolutionary period, as 'only slightly tinted with revolutionary colours' could only be prompted by the difference in national traits.

The Russians found Heinrich Brandler altogether easier to handle than Ernst. Following the March Action, Brandler went to Moscow to escape legal persecution, and there assimilated many Russian customs. He seemed, and really was, a man of action. Among all the foreign visitors he was quickest to sense Stalin's power. He greatly admired Stalin and forecast that he, not Trotsky, as was generally assumed, would be the man of the future. He even tried to imitate his manner.

During his long stay in Russia he unwittingly succumbed to the not yet openly made claim that the real Communist leadership must be left to the Russian section of the Comintern. Otherwise Brandler would hardly have considered himself equal to the role of exclusive leader of the German revolution. This attitude is revealed by a defeated, frustrated Brandler after the so-called 'German October' of 1923. He claimed the situation was highly misjudged but accepted responsibility in the belief that the Russian leaders were more experienced and their opinion more valid than his.

Brandler could easily satisfy his own ambition and play the exclusive leader chiefly because of Ernst Meyer's indifference to rank. Ernst was quite prepared to work on an equal footing with other comrades, and did not conceive of any other sort of collaboration. Yet, of all the leaders who briefly strutted on the German political scene, none was able to bear Ernst Meyer's partnership, and all tried to elbow him out of the Central Committee.

Ernst never strove for recognition. It was not only alien to his nature, but incompatible with his idea of the Party as a great donor and himself the indebted beneficiary.

'You are completely spending yourself for the Party', said a non-Party friend of his when he once returned late in the evening, very pale and tired.

'But think what the Party does for me. It elevates me from a meaningless existence and enables me to make my contribution to fulfilling a great mission.'

When Brandler returned to Germany in the winter of 1922–23, he took full advantage of his new position, and in his campaign against Ernst showed no restraint. He was playing the strong man, having acquired a taste for power in Russia. He instructed the districts, in whose hands lay the choice of the twenty-one members of the new Central Commission, to abstain from nominating Ernst (who was still officially chairman of the Politbureau). He said he did it on the authority of the Central Committee 'who believed that Ernst's re-election would be harmful to the Party'. At the Leipzig Congress in January 1923 he held secret sessions behind Ernst's back with delegates relishing intrigue and gossip. Only the well initiated understood why Ernst was being driven out of his position. It was not an open struggle, everything was done behind closed doors and Ernst Meyer made it exceedingly easy to beat him *personally*. Intrigue was not his element. It baffled him and made him childishly defenceless. He never thought of forcing matters into the open – a device he always advocated for solving Party problems – even when given full opportunity for doing so.

After Ernst delivered the political report traditionally assigned to the Chairman of the Party, the floor was taken by the Russian emissary Kleine (Guralsky). His speech used a metaphor involving bacilli: 'Unfortunately we do not have a serious Right or a serious Left. Our Right is a typhoid bacillus, and our Left a slight chill, with a varying temperature. Any doctor will confirm that a typhoid bacillus with a slight chill can be very dangerous indeed . . .'

That the 'Right bacillus' carries greater danger than the Left is one of those easily accepted fallacies. The uprisings of the first phase of the German revolution, including the Munich events, were marked by Left danger. And so were the famous July days of 1917 in Petrograd which nearly wrecked the Russian Revolution.

Ernst could dismiss these frivolous 'arguments' with sheer mockery, but he was a poor debater on *personal* issues. He said in his concluding speech: 'All these problems have been discussed so assiduously and for so long, there is nothing I can add.' As far as the delegates were concerned, this was an endorsement of the sneers and attacks, because they were so often repeated!

I do not think Ernst learned anything from this incident. In his speech at a closed session he again omitted to expose the true meaning of Kleine's remarks and was only 'sorry' they were 'confined' to personal abuse. But he gave an excellent account of his dealing with the Rathenau crisis revealing that, contrary to the accusations of indulgence towards the SPD bosses, it was he who had been rebuked by the rest of the Central Committee for harshness and only asked to conduct the negotiations when the situation demanded utmost aggressiveness.

But after countering all the attacks, he came to a truly staggering conclusion:

'Comrades', he said, 'what are the real political reasons which are causing the delegates to refuse my re-election? . . . The delegates believe that the political struggle and political clarification within the Party would be better served if the Central Committee did not include a man who could be regarded as an opportunistic element. This is a reasonable argument which could be considered.' He only demanded that the 'reasonable argument' should be 'openly proclaimed and not marred by tell-tales and gossip'. He apparently felt he had fended enough for himself, or was perhaps sorry to cause so much embarrassment. He had earlier said in one of his letters to me in July 1922 that he was 'sorry for Kleine for making himself so impossible'. He also warned his friends against any intervention on his behalf: 'The clarification of the Party is more important than the election of an individual to the Central Committee.'

The initiators of the campaign were somewhat shaken by Ernst's speech and had to change tactics: he was to be sacrificed to appease Ruth Fischer and her Berlin stronghold.

Ernst told them: 'You all know that I would accept any measure profitable to our Party', but he passionately warned against intrigues and dishonesty 'detrimental to it and to the ideals we all try to serve'. His last words and warning produced a great stir. Klara Zetkin paid Ernst tribute in her own feminine way: she got up in tears and kissed him.

Ernst was dismayed by the procedures but felt in no way beaten. He was perhaps even more self-confident and more convinced of his political powers. Those unworthy little games would be overcome with the consolidation of the Party, they were only growing pains – after all the Party was only four years old.

However, his need for support and sympathy must have been overwhelming. I had to interrupt my stay in Leipzig to be with him, but he did not expect me. The Congress closed sooner than scheduled and the delegates were already leaving when my train arrived. I had to rush to catch the departing train. Ernst looked at me as if I were an apparition from another world. He was speechless for a while, kissed me, stammered and held my hands, oblivious, it seemed, to the entire world. Radek, who shared our compartment, looked baffled, he even forgot to put on his customary sarcastic smile. It may have dawned on him how little he knew Ernst, and he spoke to him with reverence.

6.
The 'German October'

The Party was preparing for 'October', and so was the country as a whole. One part of the formula for an acute revolutionary situation seemed fulfilled: the people could not go on living as they were any longer. The mood of the country seemed to preclude any doubt that a decisive struggle was imminent.

Demonstrating the other part of the formula, that 'the upper classes are unable to rule in the old way' depended very much on the Communist Party itself. Its policy was in no way impeccable. The basic fault lay in the idea that revolutionary energy had to be spared for the 'final struggle'. Ernst argued that revolutionary ardour could not be preserved in a vacuum or put on ice. It must be kept alive and continuously nourished by a day-to-day struggle even for inadequate partial aims. The workers would not stake everything on a 'final battle' before they had tested their own strength as well as the strength and *ability* of their leadership in a succession of minor encounters *preceding* such a battle. It was particularly true of non-Communist workers whose confidence and support the Party could only hope to win by well-conceived, intensified activity. In his 'economy drive' Brandler not only failed to encourage such activity but, on various occasions, went so far as to call off actions already in progress. These tactics were applied in the early spring in the case of striking Ruhr miners, long before a definite date for the uprising was even considered. The workers suffered a number of setbacks without any attempt at resistance by the Party.

The Communists entered the SPD (Zeigner) government on 10 October 1923. The coalition was regarded as a springboard for insurrection. It was a challenge to the ruling class, and the interference of the Central government was regarded as inevitable. An elaborate programme was worked out in the best revolutionary tradition as a mode of action, and was unanimously accepted, even by the Left. It consisted of twenty points, with the chief emphasis on measures against the imminent military invasion: 'Arming of all existing defence units within ten days; mobilisation; purchase of arms by the socialist government.'

On the political side the programme demanded the 'removal of all reactionaries from leading positions and their replacement by Party members; break up of fascist dens and imprisonment of their leaders; co-ordination of the activity of factory councils and other units immediately connected with the struggle', and so on. Zeigner accepted the programme – a condition for the alliance. But his vacillations were obvious from the start: none of the decisive 'provocative' steps were even attempted.

Ernst was very apprehensive but no one ever doubted that a decisive battle lay ahead. As the time approached he started making personal arrangements, anxious to have me near, to prevent separation through a railway stoppage or other calamity in an acute upheaval. He sent me to Berlin to let our flat in order to reduce the danger of vandalism, particularly to save our rich library in case of a counter-revolutionary victory – a possibility which, of course, also had to be considered.

The zero hour came during a peaceful afternoon on 22 October. I received a telegram from Ernst to come immediately to Frankfurt. Within half an hour my suitcases were packed ready for the next train.

In the evening we went to a meeting. The hall was packed, the excitement great. We were waiting for a signal proclaiming the general strike. How familiar it was to me. I remembered the night in Munich four years earlier – it did not come off then. But at that time the Communists did not expect victory. The upheaval was thrust upon them against their will. It was different now.

Yet history repeated itself. While we waited feverishly for the 'signal', a conference of Workers' Councils was in session. No plan of action was discussed. At that late hour the conference only found the courage to discover and *admit* their tragic impotence and to sound retreat.

On 10 October five Communists had entered the Saxon government. And four days later President Ebert gave the Reichswehr General Mueller an order to occupy Saxony-Thuringia. He unearthed a fitting paragraph to 'legalise' the action. But the rank and file of his party and even higher ranks were outraged. General Mueller himself, not only the Communists, expected stiff resistance under these unprecedented circumstances.

The conference of Workers' Councils, with 469 delegates, was only summoned on 21 October. Yet the entry of the Communists into the government itself should have been made dependent on the mood of this authoritative body and on its will to fight against the expected intervention of the Reich. The other task should have been to accelerate the arming of the workers. Even that lame conference would have reacted differently had it been faced with the existence of a large number of armed workers. But Brandler was playing safe and waited for the initiative to come from 'the majority' – his socialist partners. He was afraid to break up the alliance, putting his faith in Zeigner's fighting will and power, which proved to be sheer imagination. There were neither arms – instead of the alleged 50,000 to 60,000 rifles no more than 800 (!) could be mustered at that moment – nor the resolution to find and use them, though Zeigner's government was in control of the police and available arms.

The spare resources of the Communists, all their 'Red Hundreds' might have sufficed as a supporting force in an insurrection, but were negligible in a fight against an organised army. This, of course, Brandler could have found out sooner and either tried to force the issue or sound the alarm and resign. A timely resignation would also have served as a clarion call for those non-Communist workers who were genuinely ready to defend their government by force, just as Brandler's remaining in the government lulled them into the belief that everything was fine.

There was no spirit of urgency at the Party conference. It was chiefly composed of moderate delegates equal to dealing only with current problems of workers' welfare. It was another grave oversight of the Party not to secure re-elections of the councils. This had been the first step of the Munich Communists *before* they joined the Soviet Republic. The fate of the insurrection was thus decided. Yet no one dared pronounce the death sentence, and deliberations continued on and behind the scene.

The Communists tried to save face by appealing for a general strike, but the idea fell flat. None of those present, not even Brandler himself, took it seriously. Against marching military forces a 'peaceful' weapon of this nature could have been effective in the hands of a united, organised majority, as was the case during the Kapp-Putsch, but not in the hands of the Communists against a divided SPD. Carried away by a spontaneous feeling of solidarity, the workers were known to join in a Communist-initiated struggle, but never to answer in an *organised* way a call for action against their legitimate leaders.

Couriers dispersed to sound retreat, and never before was there such a pitiful end to a great promise. Brandler called off a fight for which the workers had been preparing with all their hearts for many months. And he did it at the last moment while all the time maintaining the illusion of an imminent battle. Dazed by this unexpected turn, some of the workers tried to put up some resistance. They fought almost with their bare hands, put obstacles in the way of marching troops, threw stones and occasionally fired.

The workers were deeply ashamed of the military intervention against a legal Socialist government and called the period 'a black year'. Ruth Fischer testifies to a remarkable harmony between Communist and social-democratic workers regarding their common military defence and an excellent fighting spirit. And Thalheimer, Brandler's keenest apologist, spoke of the general revolutionary mood, with Fighting Hundreds springing up everywhere as if conjured out of thin air.

Yet only Hamburg fought on a large scale. There are conflicting versions about the origin of 'The Hamburg Barricades'. Some attribute it to a misinterpreted wave of Thaelmann's hand at the Conference, others to his explicit order: it was alleged that he had to leave the Conference at an earlier hour and, without any doubt in his mind that an insurrection would take place, gave the signal. When the news of the misunderstanding reached him ' he had not the heart to terminate the battle . . .'

Characteristically, even this abortive battle was looked upon with pride. The workers cherished the memory of 'The Hamburg Barricades', and it greatly enhanced, rather than damaged, the prestige of Thaelmann, its unwitting initiator.

On 23 October Mueller occupied Dresden. On the 27th, Berlin demanded Zeigner's abdication. Zeigner was arrested and defamed. The Communist ministers went underground. So ended the 'German October'.

A hue and cry was raised against Brandler. He, in his turn, put the blame on the Russians. Perhaps they had their share in the miscalculations. But they too were led astray. To carry favour with his high sponsors, Brandler had greatly exaggerated the revolutionary potential, particularly that of his own stronghold – Saxony-Thuringia – which according to him was just waiting to change hands. Though he afterwards complained that the reports he himself had received while in Moscow were irresponsible, unrealistic and not borne out by the facts, his faction also held the view that the situation was favourable enough if not for creating, in October, a Soviet Republic, at least for gaining an enormous influence over the masses. Thalheimer wrote that the Party resembled an army convinced of having victory safely in the bag.

When the last reckoning began in Moscow, Zinoviev explained his tactics by Brandler's firm claim that Zeigner was determined to resist the onslaught and that an army of some 50,000 to 60,000 workers was at the government's disposal. This number figured in many records. Zinoviev's much discussed telegram to ignore General Mueller and arm the Saxonian workers was composed on the basis of Brandler's evaluation and in his presence. Even if he was not directly responsible for the telegram – Zinoviev stated that Brandler only reluctantly gave his consent – its dispatch was completely justified. In fact, nothing else could have been done. To assert that Zeigner was ready to arm that number of workers was equal to guaranteeing his will to fight. It was a case of making decisions on the basis of distorted evidence.

But the Russians had more than their share of guilt by granting such unlimited authority to a man with the qualifications of, at best, a good local leader. Brandler, in return, attempted to justify their confidence and constantly looked with one eye to Russia, which even more obscured his common sense and judgement.

The workers' retreat from Brandler was as complete as his own bewildering volte-face; they were led to believe that dealings with the Social Democrats, the United Front, lead to the betrayal of the revolution !

Was it really a revolution betrayed ?

The chances of a successful Communist uprising were never seriously assessed. Too many were busy grinding their own axes to care for a proper analysis. These include even Trotsky who, to the end of his days, bluntly accused Brandler and the Comintern of 'betrayal'. As for the Left – Ruth Fischer and Maslow – they made full use of the upsurge of bitterness and indignation which led the workers to look for other leadership. The Left saw their time coming and, forgetting their own consent to the coalition, wallowed in denunciation of 'Communist ministerialism', United Front, and all.

Could it be defined as the classical revolutionary situation ?

The French occupation of the Ruhr in January, a vital industrial part of Germany, caused palpable disintegration of the bourgeoisie. The Cuno government issued an open call for strikes and passive resistance. The workers unreservedly answered the call, and the unimaginable happened – a kind of 'united front' between the workers and the ruling class. Whatever the designs of the government the situation was explosive. As in times of war, the workers felt 'wanted', they were flattered and encouraged to fight, and their self-confidence was raised. The attitude of their 'partners' who were often divided in the pursuit of their own selfish interests and ready for compromise with the invaders, was another source of radicalisation. According to the minutes of the next Party Congress, Brandler's group stated that had they correctly assessed the significance of the Ruhr conflict 'a German-Soviet Republic would be well within reach'.

But it was still in the power of the government to disrupt the movement. By the end of September passive resistance was called off and the bourgeoisie, to a great degree re-unified, was able to concentrate on the stabilisation of the mark. This was the surest means of pacifying the restless masses, indeed, the very promise of pending stabilisation could paralyse the activity of a considerable number of workers.

A retreat may have been inevitable. But not such a catastrophic and defenceless retreat. The workers were never able to find out by their own experience whether the revolution was 'betrayed' or whether they lost the battle in a square fight, not yet being strong enough to achieve their goal. They felt humiliated and cheated.

7.

Formation of the Centre Group

The swing to the left was a powerful and essentially healthy renunciation of a dangerously Right policy, and of Brandler. Yet in the stampede the Party was trampling under foot all its traditions and dearly acquired experience. In those critical days the leadership went to the so-called Centre Group – the political centre – which dominated the Central Committee until the Ninth the Frankfurt Congress in April 1924. The historians mention Koenen, Stoecker, Remmele, Ulbricht as the leaders of the Centre, but the forgotten Ernst was all the same the head of that faction and was called to Moscow to determine the new policy.

During the later reign of the Left, the Centre was conveniently labelled the Right. It was thrown into the same pot with the Brandlerists and held responsible for the October defeat. This view died hard, one might say it had not died at all. The Comintern accepted the idea and on every occasion identified Ernst, the chief protagonist of the Centre, with the Brandlerists. Even when the Comintern was compelled to call him back to the leadership, it officially called him 'the Right'. No reasoning or stern protests made any difference.

In reality the Group firmly opposed Brandler's policy and, after he joined the Zeigner government they persistently repeated: 'Our entry into the Cabinet has only one aim, to reinforce tenfold the revolutionary spirit and courage of the masses and to organise our forces'. They preached 'audacity in procuring arms' and bombarded Brandler with criticism and warnings. When he returned from Moscow they had urged him to inspect the districts and take thorough cognizance of conditions and mood *before* entering the government. The failure to follow this demand, Brandler confessed later, was his greatest error. In October 1923, they reproached Brandler for 'playing minister': 'In times of imminent struggle one should aim at arousing in the workers a spirit of defiance and self-sacrifice and not indulge in work of secondary importance, tying oneself to "governmental commitments".' On the eve of the Chemnitz Conference, 20 October, they sent him three demands to come to Berlin. He refused, still busy negotiating with the SPD, and having no time for 'advice'.

At the Frankfurt Congress of 1924, Ernst said:

> During the October days there were no differences between the basic core of the Centre and the Left ... Our will to fight was no less sincere than that of the Left. We quarrel because they treat the problem in a demagogical way – as to whether we could or could not have won ... This is not the essential point unless you are out to get votes ... Even if it would not end in victory, it was our duty to accept battle. A retreat after a square fight hand in hand with a large section of SPD workers, thus inevitably creating a cleavage between them and their leaders, is the right retreat. Retreat is also part of a struggle to win the majority of the workers. If the Party thinks such a move necessary, it must frankly face the workers and explain it to them. But we have fled from both, the battle and the workers. We should never have retreated in that way. This was not a retreat, it was a breakdown of the Party.

But it was impossible for the Centre to make up at a stroke for all of Brandler's failures and least of all to create a split at that last stage. The Party was spellbound by Brandler's authority and, of course, everybody believed that he acted in full agreement with the

Comintern. Brandler confessed that 'in moments of doubt' he always preferred 'to obey the Russian leaders'.

After Brandler's defeat, as in the aftermath of the March Action, the immediate task was to minimise panic and despair. With all its tragic errors, the movement also carried invaluable lessons for the future which were neglected in the hunt for scapegoats. The Social Democrat workers could have been taught the truth, long held by the Communists, that parliamentary victories alone are not enough to achieve socialist ends. The latest events could have served to destroy the democratic illusions so deeply ingrained in the German workers and make them more susceptible to Communist ideas.

Ernst in no way minimised the Right danger, but at that particular moment his aim was to stem the tide of hysteria spurred on by the Left and to help the Party see the events in their true perspective. Despite all the Left's errors he upheld their value in checking the strong tendencies of reformism within the German movement. He was convinced that the Left would learn through experience and remain in the leadership for good. He repeatedly stated: 'I would *of course* much rather collaborate with the Left than with the Right' – a view which he kept to the end of his days.

After many fruitless encounters of the early revolutionary years, with heavy losses of devoted, heroic workers and leaders, the Party was a shambles. In February 1920 at an early Party Congress, Brandler had remarked: 'We don't have any Party now . . . After I acquainted myself with the conditions in Rhineland-Westphalia I realised that it is worse than having no movement at all . . . and it will be impossible in the near future to put the Party on its feet.'

At that time, Ernst had taken a more optimistic view: 'The objective situation, economic and political crises, will soon dissipate the defeatist mood. The momentary exhaustion will soon be overcome, under no circumstances must we let that mood infect us.

We must co-ordinate and intensify the revolutionary forces and not give room to pessimism but concentrate on new activity.'

His speech after the October debacle was in the same spirit:

> We have the conditions for new conflicts, we are also witnessing the first counter-attacks of the proletariat and it is defeatism to say that we must first create a Communist Party to be able to fight. If, after a defeat on the October scale, the workers set out to wage even unsuccessfully large defensive battles, it is a great step forward. The fascist wave, forecast by Trotsky, appears weaker and less significant than was assumed. We must orientate the masses in the spirit of a mounting revolutionary tide.

> The Party had not anticipated the mass movement of last January in Berlin, Hamburg, Ruhr and Middle Germany. The workers had not been affected by the deep depression suffered by our Party.

The Party included some highly notable people, among them the Austrian countess Hermynia zur Muehlen, Wittfogel, the future expert on Chinese affairs; the millionaire Felix Weil; and the famous master spy, Richard Sorge.

Weil, creator and owner of an Institute for Social Research, dominated the scene. He genuinely hated his wealth which made him a kind of outcast. He was very modest in his tastes, sincere and unassuming. His happiest time, he told us, was when, as a student, no one knew of his position. He then met and married the daughter of a socialist veteran – her mother was a close friend of Klara Zetkin.

Weil's greatly cherished ambition was to create an establishment similar to the Marx-Engels Institute in Moscow, equipped with a staff of professors and students, with libraries and archives which he hoped one day to donate to a victorious German Soviet state. His father offered him a deal, agreeing to finance the costly hobby on condition that his son lived according to his means in a large mansion, butlers and all, during the old man's lifetime. The father was a very sick man and Weil accepted. The luxury embarrassed him and he was pathetically apologetic when entertaining comrades in his home. His wife played the part of 'the poor rich girl' almost convincingly.

With the death of the father Weil was free to discard his detested surroundings, but his wife refused. She had got used to her new ways and could not live without luxury and the 'really cultured people' of the Rothschild set. It hit him hard. 'More than once I gazed at the waters of our river', he told me. But he stood the test honourably, giving up wife, child and luxury and returning to the modest life of an average professional man.

Hermynia zur Muehlen, the sophisticated, witty countess, full of charm and vivacity, started her turbulent life by marrying a Baltic Baron who promised to use her considerable dowry to turn his estate into a Tolstoyan paradise. But when I came to know her she was living with her not too successful literary Jewish husband, seven years her junior, in a dismal boarding house. She was frail, supporting herself by translations and by writing stories for Communist youngsters. Three dogs were the last relics of luxury which the once spoiled eccentric lady could not resist and which added endless complications to her hard life.

The man who achieved world renown, however, was Richard Sorge. 'Ika' for short, and his wife Christiane, were both employed in Weil's Institute. His wife was proof of his reputation as irresistible to women. Married to a well-established highly respected German professor, she scorned the security of a prosperous home to follow the uncertain destinies of Ika, a student of her husband and seven years her junior.

Sorge was in his early thirties, tall with the exquisite movements of a well-built naturally elegant body, a perfect model for mythological statues – Apollo himself. There was a boyish touch in his personality, in his grey-blue twinkling eyes and his strange quiet laughter which slightly shook his whole huge frame. He was rather modest, not at all the self-assured go-getter they make of him now.

Ernst and I spent a few 'drinking bouts' in the Sorge's flat and I had the impression Ika thought it very smart to drink but did not really enjoy it. He spoke with childish rapture of the alleged drinking capacity of Stalin: 'What a man!'

At the end of 1924 the Sorges went to Moscow, she to work in the Marx-Engels Institute, he on an assignment unknown to me. I met them there in the autumn of 1925. Their marriage was breaking up and came to an end in 1926. She returned to Germany, he was sent to England. I suppose that was the beginning of activities which initiated his famous spying career.

It was on his return from England in 1929 that I saw him for the last time. He had suddenly been ordered back, pushed aside without money or explanation. He worked in England on a very dangerous assignment – something in the nature of disseminating Communist ideas in the army or getting military information. The expected punishment was around ten years of hard labour. He had to live in London in strict seclusion: no social contacts, no girl-friends: 'Just think, those long-legged slim English girls!' A punishment in itself.

In the meantime, a big shift in the Moscow oligarchy took place. Bukharin's office – Sorge's sponsors – was reshuffled, and his so dearly acquired information was, for many months, not even looked at. I do not know how he was so sure of it, perhaps he found out that the reports were not forwarded to their destination, but this discovery made him furious. I remember him pacing the room, his fists clenched: 'Those dogs, those dogs, how I hate them! This disregard for human suffering, feeling.'

He was choking with humiliation and planning all kinds of revenge: 'At least they must give me proper notice. And they have not paid me for months.'

I tried to dissuade him: 'You will have to start anew, a small sum of money, even if you succeed, will not help much.' He knew it, of course, he just lost his head.

I remember him standing in the dark passage of the gate, saying goodbye. He wanted me to go out with him. He showed too much eagerness and I refused. He tried hard: 'Final? Final?' I looked, perhaps with a certain regret, at his charming excited face: 'Sorry, yes, final.'

I locked the gate behind him . . .

Apparently somebody sensed his talents for intelligence work and singled him out for the new assignment. What made him accept it? Money, adventure, despair? It could not be his old idealism, his sincere youthful devotion to a cause. We had such splendid human material in those old days and we so relentlessly squandered it. Trotsky said something which stuck forever in my mind: 'The greatest crime of the Comintern was the corruption of those people who set out to lead humanity into a better future.'

8.

Victory of the Ultra-Left, 1924

The victory of the Left exceeded all expectations. A group of young inexperienced people with no roots in the workers' movement, hardly tested in battle, managed to rally to its side *in free unrestricted* elections – the greater number of German Communists, gaining 92 delegates as against 34 for the Centre Group. Brandler's defeat was complete.

The new revolutionary surge brought to the fore eager, impatient people, carried by their own newly acquired radicalism. Proud of their discovery that Parliament was no salvation, that trade unions were not revolutionary bodies and the Social Democrats not a revolutionary party, they fought against any collaboration with them. The pitiful collapse of the workers' government in Saxony-Thuringia seemed to justify their darkest suspicions.

They were supplemented by a new revolutionary element, the 'Red Hundreds', and other military groups who were drilled for battle and had no use or opportunity for serious theoretical study. Suspended in air after the Party's retreat they were an easy prey for almost any leadership and added a flavour of their own to the general confusion.

This time these rebels were not cast aside by the Party, but rather found encouragement and organisation from a leadership sharing their mood and ideas. A large number of Left supporters were former Independent Socialists who joined the Communists in the hope of quick results and were just as loth to deal with the tedious old organisations.

These audacious romantics wanted freedom from Moscow as well as from Berlin. One section (Boris and Samosh, both Russians) demanded a breach of all political and organisational ties between the Communists and the Russian state. Another advocated a Party structure with the Central Committee as a mere executive for the policy of various local bodies – in contrast to the existing practice where the Central Committee was assigned to work out the policy for the Party as a whole.

'Freedom' ran riot; nobody concerned himself with what would happen if ten localities worked out ten different modes of action. They called themselves and went down in history as the 'Left'. But they were in reality the protagonists of ultra-left ideas – the familiar refusal to participate in trade unions, the same negation of United Front tactics. Zinoviev understood the nature of the Left and watched the events with great alarm. But there was nothing he could do about it without making himself guilty of flagrant dictatorial interference. In those days such an attitude was unthinkable. He therefore welcomed the building of a Centre Group relying on the Party's older, more experienced men, uncompromised in the recent debacle to help the new leaders overcome their deficiencies. The core of his message to the Frankfurt party Congress in 1924 was that the new leadership could only serve the revolution by close collaboration with the Centre Group, benefiting from the experience and their best traditions. Only such collaboration could guarantee the creation of a truly revolutionary party.

Unfortunately, later, Zinoviev did not follow this policy himself.

The Party was entirely dominated by the Ruth Fischer-Maslow team and Ruth was by far the greater figure. I first heard about her from Radek who spoke in truly rapturous terms of her genius and beauty and was convinced that she would soon take the place of Rosa Luxemburg.

Of course, I was eager to meet this extraordinary woman. A young girl with a round fresh face, which made you think of a pretty chambermaid, with a figure already marked by excessive plumpness, was introduced to me by Muenzenberg. She did not yet wear proletarian disguise, rather a white woollen dress which was smart and extravagant, considering the need for frequent cleaning. I was so surprised that afterwards I repeatedly questioned Muenzenberg: 'Ruth Fischer; you mean *that* Ruth Fischer?' But, of course, I did not question her outstanding gifts. Her unusual speaking powers alone would make her a great asset to any party. Her misfortune, and even more the Party's misfortune, was that she was put into such a dominant position before she had time to mature and learn. On the other hand it is very doubtful whether she was able to accept or absorb any ideas which ran counter to her mood and inclinations. Even at that early age she seemed to think there was nothing she could learn. Ernst was sometimes quite put out by her political ignorance, claiming that she never even read the Communist Manifesto, let alone any other theoretical literature!

She had no inhibitions, no concern for truth or fair play when her interests – political or personal – were at stake. And she was terribly self-assured. Once we were sitting together at a meeting and I asked her whether she would care to mention something in her speech. I submitted my point to her as a layman would to a great scholar. But she considered it an insult to her pride and shouted: 'I do not need any coaching, comrade!'

At the end of 1922 we met socially in Moscow. The struggle between the Left and Ernst had been in progress for some time and the methods of the former did not dispose me in Ruth Fischer's favour. But she was laid up with a high temperature and I felt obliged to nurse her. We spent many hours together and again I was struck by her inflated self-assurance. She tried to be amiable but she was definitely not a woman's woman. I remember her compliment: 'They say that truly interesting women come into their own at a quite advanced age. What a future lies ahead of *us*!' I smiled to myself: What a smart way of paying *yourself* a compliment!' But at least she meant to be gracious . . .

The Left started their reign with a sweeping victory in the parliamentary elections of May 1924 with 3,700,000 votes cast for the Communists and an increase of seats from 15 to 62. The gains were even more significant since they were achieved at the expense of the SPD which lost 70 seats in the process.

Several factors contributed to the success: It was the first election after the merger with the Independent Socialists; the revolutionary mood had not entirely died out; and it was, to a large degree, an answer to the hated Reich's intervention in Saxony-Thuringia, its removal of a legitimate government and its subsequent repressions.

Though fundamentally opposed to parliamentary government, the Left conducted the campaign with great vigour. The electoral paraphernalia, with its meetings, demonstrations and parades well suited their temperament, and they were good at expounding abstract revolutionary ideas which needed neither great theoretical skill nor much experience. They had some excellent speakers on their side and, of course, the unanimous support of all Party sections.

Proud of the success, self-confident, exhilarated, a delegation of Lefts introduced themselves to Moscow and captivated it. They were more to the taste of the Russians who felt emotionally akin to this ardent, boisterous, unconventional lot, fraternising in the streets – to all appearances 'true Bolsheviks'. Thaelmann's notorious removal of his collar in the middle of a public speech brought him more popularity than his rhetoric ever could. Ruth Fischer, too, was masquerading in proletarian outfits complete with an ugly oversized Soviet Star dangling from her bosom. Her speech at the Red Square created a real sensation. The Lefts were altogether familiar figures and two of their foremost leaders, the Russian Maslow and the highly gifted Heinz Neumann spoke Russian. A spontaneous feeling of kinship swept everyone off his feet, including the head of the Comintern, Zinoviev. This may be one explanation for his subsequent attitude towards the Left. It is also possible that he succumbed to wishful thinking, and tried to persuade himself that the flame of revolution might be kindled again by the new leadership and that all was not lost. He started priding himself on his unity with the Left and joined in their excessive baiting and victimisation of opponents. He not only condoned, but personally took part in crushing the Centre, the group he himself had singled out for the new leadership.

The Left emerged as a supreme power and was resolved to consummate its victory to the full. A reign of intimidation and reprisals was inaugurated, and they were years ahead of the Russians in introducing such practices as shunning comrades who had fallen from favour. Prominent Mensheviks were still admitted to responsible positions in Soviet institutions in Russia, but the German Left demanded that all vacancies in Russian institutions in Germany be reserved only for their favourites. They anticipated the vulgarisation of political terminology by their Bolshevik masters, using the word 'bolshevisation' in appeals for improving daily work long before Stalin started branding petty thefts in factories as 'Bukharinism'. Expulsions of the Right had already started in July 1924 and by the end of the year the Left went so far as to expel Party members for 'casting suspicion on leading personalities of the Party'.

Whereas the Soviet leadership still tolerated dissent and criticism, the Left in Germany rapidly abolished all Party democracy. Under pretence of saving money and cutting down the Party apparatus, they cleared it of nearly all 'undesirables'. Members of the Right or Centre, however qualified, had little chance of being employed in a Russian institution in Germany. I was one of the very few exceptions and, owing to my name, was allowed to slip through the tight net.

Financial difficulties soon beset the Party and a whispering campaign, with accusations of embezzlement found, characteristically, open ears first of all among the top leaders. The scuffle for coveted positions caused so much corruption and mistrust among them that they were ready to believe the worst.

Unfortunately, our circles were also buzzing with ugly rumours. Ernst explained the financial difficulty by a disproportion between published and consumed propaganda: piles of unwanted 'bolshevisation' sheets could easily lead to financial bankruptcy. The Left went too far in their 'revolutionary drive'. As early as 1918, Ernst had argued that it was useless to print more propaganda than could be disseminated: 'The size of our organisation limits our capacity to reach greater numbers of readers. Rotting balls of paper, even inscribed with the most fiery revolutionary script, only waste space and money.'

The Left was particularly fierce in denouncing the blackmailing pressure of the 'rouble' which allegedly caused the destruction of the healthy German revolutionary movement. The budget was concocted 'with an eye on Moscow and an effort to gain favour with the authorities on whom the grants depended; its single items tended to comply with the given Russian policy', wrote Ruth Fischer.

Double-crossing, lies became daily practice under the Left. This was, of course, accompanied by persecution of intellectuals. Any leader, determined to stifle opposition, treats polemics, discussions, even knowledge itself as sinister creations of a distorted intellectual mind and as diversions from urgent revolutionary tasks. It is a device calculated to appeal to the primitive feelings of the workers and to flatter them – invented by intellectuals.

It all went under the cover of 'bolshevisation'. They denied that the West European revolutionary movement, including the Spartakists, had any merit – the Bolsheviks alone held the revolutionary monopoly. The word 'Bolshevism' was used nearly as often then as the word 'Stalin' was later.

It was a hard time even if we were spared the worst. Ernst was the number one target for attacks. He was not elected to the new Central Committee, his criticisms and proposals were answered with abuse, he was stamped as 'Right' and seriously faced expulsion. In the end he was dismissed as the editor of a non-Party evening paper, *Die Welt am Abend*.

Fear of political reprisals, and of losing favour with the rulers, seized the Party. A new element was introduced – people started shunning real or even suspected dissenters. Once W.

Koenen quickly turned away from Ernst when Ruth Fischer was approaching. Ernst laughed all the way home in anticipation of my violent reaction to the story. The Soviet Embassy also fell in line with the new practices. Krestinsky, the Ambassador, hastily stopped inviting Ernst (and of course me) to formal receptions, though he never stopped seeking Ernst's opinion in private.

The atmosphere among our own political friends was also becoming unsavoury. Gossip, cynical tales and self-righteousness were mounting. It was not always easy to keep clear of this mood, and we sometimes caught each other doing fundamentally the same – making not very flattering remarks about nearly everybody. But at least we were aware of the danger: 'Careful, with everybody at fault, only the two of us would be spared.'

We were saved by a steady influx of Russian visitors who were, characteristically, much more courageous than their German opposite numbers or the Soviet old-timers. The most remarkable was Jaglom, at 26 a deputy of Tomsky, the chairman of the powerful Soviet trade unions and editor-in-chief of its central organ, *Trud*. Together with Bukharin and Tomsky he put up a fight in 1928 against Stalin's course of industrialisation and collectivisation and also against the re-introduction of an ultra-left policy in Germany. A deep friendship developed between Ernst and Jaglom and the Russians brought much gaiety into our life. On Christmas Eve Jaglom brought a party of three deputy ministers who were on an official visit to Germany. They were entertained by the German Foreign Office which was tactless enough to end the reception with the German national anthem. The guests had, of course, to get up and listen in all solemnity. But before they had time to sit down again, the Russians sang their national anthem, and the hosts, to their consternation, had to listen to the 'Internationale' in the same solemn manner.

A great part in the life of the Party was played by the *Roter Frontkaempfer Bund* (Red Front Fighters League) – the RFB – which became a great asset to the Left at the end of 1924 and filled a glaring gap created by a policy of abstention from political work. The League had its roots in the Communist military formations of 1923. When the revolution failed, it took on the task of protecting meetings, workers' houses and Party premises as well as individuals from monarchist gangs that terrorised the big cities. It soon blossomed into a huge organisation which, for a while, successfully competed with the monarchist *Stahlhelm* (Steel Helmet) and similar groups which hoped to revive the military spirit.

League members were clothed in smart uniforms and all the Party demanded in return was that they should parade and attend meetings. It was much more attractive 'to serve the revolution' this way than to perform tedious routine Party work, and the League attracted workers far beyond Communist circles – SPD members and even some Catholics could be found in its ranks. Thaelmann was chosen as its president.

With propaganda as the Party's new and only purpose the League added glamour to countless meetings and demonstrations. It appeared everywhere, attracted crowds with music and songs, not unlike the Salvation Army, and performed services similar to those of boy scouts. During a flood catastrophe they earned well-deserved acclaim for their disciplined selfless assistance. The appeal of the young uniformed men marching in military formations, with bands playing and banners flying, was tremendous. Their annual rally in Berlin, with clenched fist salutes and shouts of 'Red front' and 'Heil Moscow', became a national event. People of various political beliefs cheerfully gave hospitality to tens of thousands of strangers who poured in from the provinces. The town was on its feet, people cheered and offered refreshments. I heard from a reliable source that Trotsky, on a clandestine visit to Berlin in the summer of 1926, watched their procession and raved about the incompetence of a Party which, with such an army, was no closer to revolution.

With the spread of unemployment people lost the mood for playing soldier, and the popularity of the RFB faded. Their disbanding in May 1929 went almost unnoticed. Ostensibly created to counteract the revival of the military spirit, they themselves grew, without serious military training, into militarists of a kind. Gradually they degenerated and scores of them went over to Hitler.

9.

Beginning of Ultra-Left Defeat

The Dawes Plan, accepted in August 1924, imposed new burdens on Germany. The recent Communist defeat brought undisguised cynicism and much 'frank talk' about leaving to die those superfluous people who burdened the country's economy – some fifteen million – in order to save it.

But the Left, reared in an acute revolutionary mood, proved incapable of adjusting itself to the new situation. The Party, which on the eve of 1923 had become a power to reckon with and was considered fit to enter a final contest for state power, built its strength in a prolonged and consistent application of United Front tactics. To achieve their ultimate aim the Communists had to win over the majority of organised workers who were still in the Social Democrat camp. There was no other way. Outside the Communist Party no better, no more class-conscious workers were to be found. It was a particularly difficult task because the SPD could claim positive contributions to workers' welfare with respect to housing, education, medical and children's care and even, to a degree, better wages and working conditions. The Communists could claim no such achievements so far. They now had to convince the workers that, even prior to the revolution, they would better protect their interests. I was often reminded by Ernst that 'we need the social democratic and trade union workers. We will either win them or there will be no revolution'. But the new leadership had no use for any agreements with the SPD and refused on principle to deal with the practical problems of the day. For them the fight for higher wages was futile, the capitalists would always find ways of eliminating the gains. Only the dictatorship of the proletariat could put an end to poverty.

The Left had won 62 seats but they were resolved to use the parliament exclusively as a propaganda arena and 'a means of disorganising the capitalist state'. They scorned any idea of positive work: 'It is not our business to teach the bourgeoisie how to solve their problems. Let them extricate themselves from their calamity.' They limited their parliamentary activities to catcalls and occasional skirmishes. Great care was taken to demonstrate their 'truly revolutionary' contempt for bourgeois institutions. They shouted abuses like 'Racketeer Republic' and made noises with sirens. They tried to humour their electors with childish practices like wrapping their hands in red cloth when taking their oath. Ruth Fischer began her maiden speech by addressing the House: 'Most Honourable Monkey-Theatre!'

The preservation of the revolutionary spirit was declared the chief objective of the movement. A new revolutionary wave was allegedly round the corner and the Party had to be ready to bring the struggle to a victorious conclusion. No one dared make a sincere analysis of the situation. To suggest a long revolutionary perspective was dangerous, such views were tantamount to pessimism and Right deviation.

An inevitable consequence was the exodus from the socialist-dominated trade unions, the very dens of reformism and treachery. The Left asserted that the German workers had not lost their faith in those decaying old bodies; it would be a mistake to waste energy trying to pump new life into them. While the Frankfurt Convention was still in session the Left formed a new organisation of 'Militant Trade Unions'. They were now left to themselves in all their revolutionary purity but in complete isolation from the struggling masses. With all their imposing initial gains and numbers, they ceased to play any part in the destiny of the country. Their activities were reduced to semi-military parades, meetings and demonstrations. Shouting and high-sounding words were substituted for militancy and, of course, there were many brawls with quite heavy casualties on the Red side.

The result of the Left's abstention policy was an immense loss of votes. In the short interval between May and December of 1924 the Party lost nearly a million votes in the new Reichstag election. Just as swift was the recovery of the SPD, with a gain of 1¼ million votes. The Party itself was dwindling with no less rapidity – from some 300,000 members at the time of the Frankfurt Congress it decreased to 121,000 members. Even allowing for the post-revolutionary ebb, the decline was alarming.

The Left tried to shrug off the parliamentary defeat; their foremost theorist, Professor Rosenberg, declared that it was of no importance whether the Party lost one or two million votes in the 'parliamentary monkey-game'. The only task was the preservation of the revolutionary spirit and the revolutionary organisation.

Ernst protested to the representative of the Executive:

Berlin, 3 January 1925

Dear Comrade,

The unprecendented passivity of the Party compels me to submit to your attention the following facts:

Almost the entire Central Committee has gone abroad leaving the party without any directions.

The Party lives exclusively on scandals which originate in the corruption of the SPD and the bourgeoisie.

The most important current political problem is solving the governmental crisis. The bourgeoisie adjourned the matter until the end of the 'holidays'. The *Rote Fahne* did them the favour of not dealing with it either. When the question was resumed on 31 December not a word was said about our demand for a Workers' and Peasants' Government. This very title is still taboo in the Communist Party. In its issue of 6 December 1924, *Hallescher Klassenkampf* took it on itself arbitrarily to substitute the words of an official proclamation of the Executive, 'Government of Workers and Toiling Peasants' by 'Dictatorship of all Toiling Masses in Town and Country'.

The Ministry has prepared the new tax and duty proposals for the coming Reichstag. The Party has no propaganda with which to combat the intricate manoeuvres of the SPD. The *Rote Fahne* published one appropriate article on 17 December . . .

This article remained an oasis in the desert. No propaganda preceded or followed it up. And those demands which I had been advocating for a long time have been criticised as 'Maslow's little deviation'.

Between February and March shop steward elections will take place. The proclamation of the *Rote Fahne* of 24 December demands 'the Red united front of the proletariat from below'.

It gives no answer to the practical question concerning our attitude towards SPD fellow-workers in the trade unions (joint trade union lists) and thus aggravates the confusion.

The districts still obey the old, incorrect instructions.

In important industrial branches (Ruhr District, mining and metal industries) a movement for higher wages has been in progress. The *Vorwaerts* deals with it on page 4 among trade union affairs. The *Rote Fahne* either ignores the matter or likewise gives it attention only in a hidden corner. The Party is not the leader of this movement and has no influence on it.

Since May 1924 we have had a steadily mounting wave of rising prices. Instead of making it an object of daily concern, the Party ignores this important aspect. The high prices are another veiled form of inflation. The Party believes in the fake stabilisation of the mark and uses it as a comfort for its setbacks.

As long as a United Front campaign on the economic and political field is not made a reality, a United Front at a trade union le-

vel remains a mere scrap of paper. The English argument
is excellent. It may supplement but not replace the German
one.
I request that you use all your influence to remedy this situation.

With comradely greetings
Ernst Meyer

The Communists were facing situations that demanded
great flexibility. Prussia had a socialist government under Otto
Braun's premiership. It maintained itself through the support of
the Centre and the Democrats who were willing to build a Republi-
can block against the ascendent monarchists. It had a small majority and could easily tumble. Its fate depended on Communist support.

No less decisive was the Communist stand in the forthcoming presidential elections. It was customary for the various parties
to present their own candidates in a preliminary run – a campaign
for testing forces. But the loss of another million votes for the Communist candidate, Thaelmann, was an unmistakable indication of
the popular feeling against a separate candidacy in the decisive run.
The situation was aggravated by the death of the socialist candidate,
Ebert. When the extreme Right put up old Field-Marshal Hindenburg no other single candidate was popular enough to carry a majority against him. The fate of the election was thus in the hands of the
Communists, and the issue could not be dodged: support a socialist
candidate or allow the election of a monarchist.

Maslow made an appeal to support a socialist candidate,
but the conditions he attached to the offer seemed more calculated
to secure a refusal. Ruth Fischer writes that '. . . the offer came so
late as to make it impossible for the SPD to change their policy – it
was rather meant as an alibi against accusations of putting Hindenburg into the saddle.'

There was full agreement among the Left leaders for sabotaging a united action with the SPD. Thaelmann was put up for the
second, decisive run.

The SPD made an attempt to secure an anti-monarchist majority, withdrawing their candidate in favour of the Centre, the Roman Catholic, Marx. It was a desperate but fruitless step since a majority could only be reached by an alliance of proletarian against bourgeois forces. The split secured Hindenburg's victory. The workers, also the Communist 'rank and file', were more realistic and knew that a victory of the opposite camp would inevitably result in more pressure on their living standards and political liberties. There was an uproar in the factories but the policy was not revised.

The support of a socialist candidate was closely bound with a chain of other, essentially United Front measures, which were categorically eliminated from the programme of the Left. The Comintern pressed for restoration of work within the old trade unions, as a basis for contact with the SPD. Despite his illusions about the Left, Zinoviev never abandoned his belief in using United Front tactics. Unlike a number of leaders, who regarded it as a means of exposing the SPD's failures or clever manoeuvres, he regarded this strategy as a positive contribution, in the interest of the workers. I heard him in Leningrad passionately refuting the idea of 'frightening off the SPD' with unacceptable demands: 'On the contrary, our demands must be popular, workable, *difficult* to reject. We need, we want collaboration. It is a step towards our aim. We must only be careful to take the initiative and not plod behind.'

Ruth Fischer played her old game; she was quite in favour of the idea while she was in Moscow: 'Everyone agreed that we should have influence in the trade unions and that we don't have it.' Back home, however, she presented every 'reason' for sabotaging the decisions:'The fate of German labour will not be decided by trade union work but by creating a political climate in which united action would be manifestly in the interest of the German workers and not merely of the "Russian State" . . . The work would only lead to a dead end, better concentrate on independent trade unions to fight the old ones in the open and break their monopoly of labour control.'

When the pressure of the Comintern proved too great the Left tried to 'outsmart' the Russians by ostensibly expelling the most ardent anti-trade unionists while maintaining 'excellent rela-tions' with them on the side. They were, in Maslow's view, 'the best elements of the Party'.

No one expected the Left to put up Ernst Meyer as a candi-date at the new elections. However, their favoured choice suddenly went over to the SPD, and the Left had to be careful since Ernst was very popular in East Prussia. The case was submitted to the Comint-ern which decided to leave the choice to the discretion of Ernst's constituency. The leaders of the local branches were summoned and a special emissary dispatched from Berlin with the explicit task of preventing Ernst's nomination. But the conference voted in his favour. He sent me a very cheerful telegram but soon guessed that his victory was too much for the Left to swallow and, therefore, too 'dangerous'. Indeed, it did not prevent Ruth Fischer from cancell-ing his mandate. Ernst demanded an explanation and she declared: 'Your name is a programme. We cannot afford to give you a promi-nent position.'

At this point, Ernst wrote to the Comintern Executive:

Berlin, 5 November 1924
Dear Comrades
The Central Committee had decided to leave the choice of parliamentary candidates to the East Prussian Party Conference.
As far as I was concerned the Central Committee decided to
use all its influence to stop the district from approving my
re-election.
In spite of strong criticism of my political activities by the Central
Committee emissary, the Conference was forced to conclude that my views in no way contradicted the resolutions
of the Comintern. I want to confirm here that my much-de-
bated views on the 'Workers' Government' were . . . identical to that of the Fifth World Congress.
After they had acquainted themselves with the situation, 9 of 13

delegates, whom the Central Committee had persuaded to sign a counter-proposal, voted in my favour. I was then nominated almost unanimously with some 60 votes against 4, as the leading candidate. Nevertheless, the Central Committee annulled the decision of the District Committee after its attempts to suspend the decision of the Conference had failed.

In addition, the Central Committee forbade me to visit East Prussia. They even hurriedly cancelled electoral meetings, which I was to address at the request of the District Committee.

The Central Committee is unable to present a single instance where I went against the resolutions of the Party or Comintern. My victimisation results solely from the necessary criticism which I made of political issues within the appropriate Party channels. The prevention of my parliamentary activity . . . signifies the beginning of my complete banishment from Party work . . . I request the Executive to examine the political reasons of the Central Committee and to give its views on the subject without delay.

In her book, Ruth Fischer alleges that Ernst later became reconciled with the Left: 'Though he maintained his fundamental position and remained loyal to his faction, after the 1923 experience Meyer had revised his estimate of the Left-wing and sympathised with their drive for independence from Moscow.'

In fact, it was Ernst's greatest pride that he was never involved in any compromises with the Left. In a 1925 note he says: 'The allegation of Comrade Fischer that Comrades Scholem and I, Froelich and Becker share the same views, base our judgement on the same assumptions and arrive at the same conclusions will not be taken seriously by a single member of the whole Party – and not by Comrade Ruth Fischer herself.'

This is further explained in a letter written to a 'Comrade Fischer' (unrelated to Ruth):

Berlin, 5 January 1925

Dear Comrade Fischer,

. . . The basis of any agreement lies in the following: How do you explain that in the winter 1923 the Party members rejected Brandler in a *free* discussion?

Further: why have neither the 'Right' nor the 'Centre' succeeded – even at the *beginning* of last year when expulsions were not yet practised – to keep or gain any districts?

Anyone who fails to see these *facts* as a partly legitimate and partly comprehensible reaction to the October policy will also be incapable of a correct evaluation of future developments.

Secondly: no truly Bolshevist opposition will emerge within a reasonable period without the help of the Executive, unless the present leadership proves to be a total failure in action. I feel too responsible towards the Party to indulge in malicious anticipation of such a collapse or in a desire to witness it.

Without the influence of the Executive (in matters of United Front policy and freedom for necessary criticism) there can be no successful opposition.

Of course, it is necessary to take part in *all* Party work, particularly in factory cells, etc.

Of course, it is also necessary to create a *homogeneous* Bolshevist opposition within the Party. The declarations of Brandler and Thalheimer and the 'right' factional material sent from Remscheid, make me feel rather sceptical.

Once, in Leipzig, I let myself be hood-winked by Brandler without offering any resistance. It is not in the interest of the Party that I should go through a similar experience again. An agreement with me can only be achieved on *my platform*. Besides, ever since Frankfurt, I have always been let down. Who among the 'Right' has ever taken a firm stand at the Editors' and Secretaries' Conferences, or even supported me?

I urgently advise Westermann or others, who find themselves in the same position, to appeal *at once* to the Executive . . . I shall write again after the session of the Central Commission.

Best regards to your wife,
Ernst Meyer

Ernst tried to use his unaccustomed leisure time for writing *The History of the Spartakus League.* I urged him to take leave and devote himself entirely to the book, but his ties with the movement were too strong; he had to be on the spot, in steady communication with the Party.

A frequent visitor at that time was Gerhart Eisler, Ruth Fischer's brother and a follower of Walter Ulbricht. He was then in his early twenties, highly intelligent, even with a touch of brilliance, erudite and witty. Unfortunately his gifts were matched by an overwhelming, embarrassing conceit. Perhaps he was trying to make up for his short flabby figure, round baby-face, and balding reddish head. His flamboyant, self-confident manner exercised a paralysing effect on people, and sometimes he could get away with murder.

The Eisler family said that they were extremely devoted to each other, but this did not prevent Ruth from denouncing Gerhart to the US House Committee on Un-American Activities during the McCarthy period, after which he was arrested, expelled as a dangerous Russian spy and delivered to Ulbricht in East Germany. The remarks I heard Eisler make about his sister after he joined Ernst's opposition were less dangerous to her, but hardly affectionate. Hearing of the accidental death of a comrade, he exclaimed: 'Couldn't it have been my little sister? Of course, I would have wept, but how very gladly.'

With the increasing failures of the Party, Russian emissaries came to sound out Ernst. On one occasion the question arose whether the opposition felt strong enough to take over the leadership. Eisler jumped to his feet: 'Who us? Who are we? Nobody! It is a ridiculous idea, we must decline.' It was an appalling statement. No opposition has a right of existence unless it is convinced of its ability to do better. Perhaps Eisler felt that he personally was not cut out for the role and grew restless.

After the removal of the Left from power he did some good work and quickly grew in stature and maturity. But in 1928 he was whisked off to China. This was designed as a means of dispersing the Centre Group of the Party, now called 'Conciliators'. A confused, unhappy young man was to assume responsible leadership in an alien country with no knowledge of language, people, conditions. He accepted the assignment and he had a comforting little formula: 'You cannot fight a sixth of the universe'. He was recalled in 1931 and given a post in Moscow. I met him there on my last visit at the end of 1932, when he was heading for a mission in West Europe. A crushed, subdued man, he gleefully admonished me: 'If you cannot lie and swindle in favour of the Soviet Union now, when it is in such danger, you have never been a Communist.'

At this time I was going to be interviewed by the head of the Comintern Propaganda Department, Gussev, about a controversial article I had written, which did not fit Stalin's command to pull to pieces all revolutionary parties to the glory of Bolshevism. I refused to make alterations and offered to withdraw the article. I was sent from one authority to the other, Gussev being the last. Eisler warned me: 'Don't fight. It will lead you nowhere. The time will come when historic truth will be restored. It does not matter now, everything must be done in favour of Soviet Russia.'

'But it means abusing the Spartakists; Leviné had given his life and Ernst the best years of his in the Party's service. Why write articles at all? I shall never put my name to falsifications.'

I returned in triumph. Gussev accepted my version! Eisler was stunned. For a while he paced the room in silence. Then: 'They gave in because . . . they don't regard you as a leader.'

After the incident, Eisler avoided my company. I last saw him in Paris in 1934 and we arranged a meeting. He never turned up.

10.

The Zinoviev Letter

The 1925 annual Party congress was due to take place in July. It was to thrash out views and determine successive policy, and was traditionally preceded by preconvention discussions which inevitably precluded a certain amount of criticism.

Ernst was besieged with warnings from well-wishers: 'Don't expose yourself. Wait. The Party needs you.' He was tempted with promises, not of posts – no one would be so clumsy as to try to bribe Ernst – but of readjustments and changes: 'Just be quiet, the Comintern will straighten everything out.'

Together with P.Froelich Ernst wrote an open letter to the Party. They did not have delegate status; the rally consisted of hand-picked men; hardly any dissident had a chance to penetrate the thick mesh. Thus there was great surprise when Ernst was allowed to follow up the open letter with a twenty minute speech, for no one knew of the secret wrangle already taking place between the Comintern and Ruth Fischer. The audience, mostly newcomers, who met the most hated man after Brandler for the first time, was polite and fairly responsive. Its very attention could be regarded, under the circumstances, as a great success.

When I read an account of the speech in *Die Welt am Abend* – Ernst's own paper – there was a dry, confused report so that no reader could make head or tail of his ideas. He had assigned the matter the space normally allotted to political reports in an evening paper, and, in the bargain, left it to a third-rate journalist. Ernst could work out the right programme, he could make a commendable speech, but it never entered his mind to gear his work for the appropriate propaganda effect. The failure was born out of his great integrity, but it was a failure harmful to his career and the Party.

The congress seemed a sheer triumph for the Left. Ruth Fischer could rightly boast that for the first time in the Party's existence the same leadership was chosen in two successive elections. The event was celebrated by a glamorous show with herself as its undisputed star, entering the meeting flanked by a smartly uniformed Red Front detachment who solemnly escorted her to a platform covered with posters and banners and took their stand behind her. That excellent orator excelled herself amidst cheers and ovations of the huge audience.

Yet, despite all the spectacle it was Ruth Fischer's swansong. Something was in the air, almost imperceptible little signs that something was amiss. Ernst received friendlier smiles and Heinz Neumann came running to greet us, speaking to me in Russian, overwhelming me with questions about health, plans – I could not remember ever having spoken to him before. I nearly asked what business it was of his, but thought no answer contemptuous enough.

No one expected decisive changes. With an ostensibly homogeneous Left leadership from the Central Committee to the last local functionary, what earthly power could oppose them? Nonetheless, in her confidential talks with the Executive Ruth Fischer curiously condemned the ultra-left and claimed that her struggle against it dated from as far back as the Frankfurt Congress of 1924. She indicted them for the greatest sin of all – opposing bolshevisation. Scholem and Rosenberg, the most prominent protagonists of the ultra-left were demonstratively excluded from the district Party administration and she even threatened her friends with 'severe measures'. She did what she could to retain her power. Ernst mockingly defined her attempts at change as 'a bad imitation of the Centre policy'. There could be no middle way between the Centre, fighting on two fronts against right and ultra-left, and Ruth Fischer. The Centre was, after all, the Left of the party.

Ruth Fischer's dilemma was to resign a position of supreme power and accept a position appropriate to her size. Power would inevitably be restored to the Centre and to Ernst Meyer. This is why she focused all her venom on Ernst, never conceiving that she would have to cede power in fact to Thaelmann.

The Tenth Congress of July 1925, was assigned to realise all the agreements the Party and the Comintern had concluded in amicable talks. In a letter to the Congress Zinoviev showered his praise on the Left leadership: 'The Communist Party built up a firm leadership; it successfully exposed and then overcame its Right deviations and simultaneously opposed those of the ultra-left; the basic core of the Central Committee was pursuing the correct course and deservedly enjoys the confidence of the Party. The Comintern unconditionally supports this core and will work hand in hand with them.'

Zinoviev reprimanded the Party very mildly for not having heeded his warnings against the ultra-left, for which he had chosen only three culprits – Rosenberg, Scholem and Katz. But he found an excuse for the mistake: 'The Party was for a time in a state of ultra-left fever. The Tenth Congress must free itself from it once and for all.' Scholem was then in a position to retort that until May, they were all, Ruth Fischer, the other comrades, and himself, affected by the ultra-left fever.

Now that the leadership was stabilised, it could afford more freedom of discussion, a change of its attitude to the opposition and a revision of the expulsions. Zinoviev had not forgotten though to demand more concentration on trade union and United Front work.

The Comintern here displayed a remarkable confusion between promises (often enough cast to the wind before) and actual achievements, for which it credited the Party in advance. It had to pay dearly for its naive complacency and self-assurance. The Congress ended in an uproar with delegates in open rebellion against the Comintern. Enraged, the Comintern demanded a representative delegation to clear up the position. By flatly refusing this, the leadership overrated its powers – the Comintern proved stronger. Under pressure several leaders decided to comply with the wishes of the Executive, and in August 1925, seven of them headed by Ruth Fischer, Thaelmann and Dengel, arrived in Moscow.

Thaelmann and Dengel were soon 'won over'. Ruth Fischer resorted to her old methods and even tried to play the fool; reprimanded for breaking her promise to build the long overdue trade union department, she said she was not aware that it was a binding agreement. She otherwise expressed her complete solidarity with the proposed changes: 'They expressed all we have been fighting for during the last two years . . . We have no basic differences about the tasks of the Party.' The instigators of the incorrect policy were really the rank and file, she declared, and she was helpless against their ultra-left moods.

Zinoviev learned his lesson and was no longer prepared to rely on verbal agreements. He proposed to put them into plain words in an open letter to the Party. Ruth Fischer was cornered. She could not very well refuse her signature to a document which allegedly expressed her own aspirations and would only facilitate her struggle against the unruly rank and file. (She later described the act as 'signing my own death sentence'.)

By the end of August, Zinoviev's Open Letter reached the German Party. Coming out of the blue it caused sensation and panic, raising speculations about Zinoviev's motives. Many agreed that it resulted from his own factional difficulties at home. In fact he was squeezed between two bitter alternatives, but had to act. Selfish motives ran parallel with the vital interests of the Party. To avail himself honourably of the dilemma he had to sacrifice his personal interests. He did not dare tell the truth. Having gone too far in his support of the Left a straightforward, clear admission of his mistakes would mean his complete undoing. Thus he tried to limit the damage to his prestige through ruse and trickery. The departure from a policy branded as a danger to the revolution was to be achieved by the dismissal of a few arbitrarily picked leaders.

Up to that point Zinoviev could be accused of errors of judgement but not of crude, irresponsible manipulations. But the Open Letter was a cynical disregard of truth and an affront to common sense and feeling. All its correct arguments were nullified by its attempt to shift the responsibility for all errors from the Party to a few individuals. To stress the point that the Party, which meant the Left, was in perfect order, Zinoviev made an absurd division between 'the sound proletarian membership and the ruling leadership' – as if the members, not the leaders, were on trial. And again he vouched, in advance: 'The Left will assert itself . . . by convincing wider and wider sections of Party members and by developing energetic, positive activity.' To cast off the guilt of his long indulgence towards the Left, he went out of his way to praise its great merits: 'It had drawn the conclusion from October 1923; it defeated Brandlerism and unified the divided Party at the time of its gravest crisis and it has to fulfill a great historic task, in spite of all past and present errors.'

Thaelmann, a faithful follower of Ruth Fischer, who never displayed a policy of his own and was won over by flattery and subtle intimidation, was chosen to lead the Party to its triumphant finale. Zinoviev even declared that the Comintern had hesitated so long because the Left leadership included a man of Thaelmann's calibre.

Was the letter beneficial to the German Party ? Dismayed and disappointed as Ernst was, he still welcomed it: 'It will hasten clarification. Whatever its ambiguities it indicates the right road. It is now *our* task to do the rest . . . It would be foolish on our part to deny Thaelmann our wholehearted support, when the Central Committee genuinely accepts the new course. We must help the Party to overcome the present crisis with the least amount of damage . . . We could not refuse to collaborate, for this was the policy we ourselves have been advocating for a long time.' It was the last time he gave the Comintern any credit or paid it homage.

Yet he did not accept the Letter unconditionally. The Secretariat of the ECCI reported: 'The Ernst Meyer-Froelich group introduced a platform of their own at the Conference of Political Secretaries and Editors. They see in the Letter a justification of their policy. They accept the Letter but do not give up their factional activities for the following reasons:

1) They do not regard the new leadership adequate enough to conduct the new course of the Executive.

2) They hold that the practical aims of the Party are not correctly defined and consider it their task to amend them.

This is characterised by Ernst Meyer's argument at the Conference: "The Party must revise its attitude towards the Dawes Plan."

This group is now engaged in great activity. It considers that the present situation is only a transitional one and hopes by energetic work to obtain the leadership of the Party.'

No one doubted that Ernst's star was rising. His letters from this period testify that this was a predominant view:

Berlin, September 1925

I received a nice letter this morning from an acquaintance, who is now in a penitentiary:

'Ruth Fischer and Maslow were only temporary leaders born out of a situation which demanded a radical approach. Since 1924 the situation has changed so much that we have to return to the tactic of the United Front. Now I wait each day for the news that *you* have taken over the Party leadership.'

... Grete St. also greeted me as 'the future Party boss' to which she, however, still added some of her ultra-left warnings. This is the *general* mood and therefore explains their particularly savage attacks on me.

Koenigsberg, 27 October 1925

Of course Koenigsberg was again a political victory for me. My resolution was accepted by 20 votes to one. In addition I was elected as a delegate to the Reichs-Conference. In two districts they accepted even more outspoken resolutions . . . The Deputy of the Executive intended to fix a session to discuss my immediate election into the Central Committee, but it had to be postponed to the middle of the week because of my journey.

Koenigsberg, 4 November 1925

. . . for the moment it is I who does the 'Slaughtering'. [Left expression for describing dealings with the opposition. RL-M.] But they still campaign against me. I must appear here more frequently.

Leaders like Muenzenberg and Heinz Neumann started flocking to seek Ernst's favours, forgiveness, excelling in crude flattery and self-abasement. Neumann confessed errors but pleaded extenuating circumstances – he was so young, he promised correction and loyal collaboration. He was quite prepared to work against his former associates and to champion the opposite views. He only wanted to maintain his leadership position.

Muenzenberg's position was more stable; he offered his loyalty in other ways – sleeping-car tickets, generous fees for *unwritten articles*: 'Just give a sketch of your ideas and your signature. I promise an expert presentation.' When I was laid up with tuberculosis in a Swiss sanatorium he became particularly persistent: 'You need money so badly, why do you refuse?' His wife, Babette Gross, went out of her way to give me work and, in her eagerness, sent me a book which had been translated before. But we did need my well-earned money and I accepted the pay.

Ruth Fischer's ambiguous behaviour set a pattern for the majority of the ruling section, and acceptance of the Zinoviev

Letter was thus secured. Yet matters did not proceed smoothly, for Berlin-Brandenburg, Ruth Fischer's stronghold, and a number of other districts, put up violent resistance. In the summer of 1926, the various groups of the Left still claimed a quarter of the Party functionaries and the struggle raged until the end of the year.

But the Left was not united. Filled with deep suspicion against anything which smacked of the 'Right', unprincipled and vague in outlook, they split in several sections. Yesterday's 'bolshevisors' now competed with each other in wild denunciations of the Soviet state. Korsch called it 'Red Imperialism'; Schwarz, who split with him, accused him of being a 'new Lenin', hitherto a term of greatest distinction. One of them, Katz, declared that 'the Soviet Union turned from the bastion of world revolution into the bastion of world-capitalism . . . The proletariat will have to fight it no less than English and German capitalism.' He accused the KPD of advocating war credits, raising Hinbenburg's revenue and so on. Such ravings only compromised the Left's cause and contributed to their disintegration. Their influence was dissipating as quickly as it had been imposed on the German body politic.

The difficulty now facing the Party was not to defeat the ultra-left, but to overcome the obstacles which were put in its way by the ambiguities of the Open Letter. After the leading group had gone through the ritual of recantation behind the closed doors of Moscow conference-halls, and a few wordy, non-committal declarations, the Left saw no compulsion to seriously revise their views, and were partly even afraid of doing so. The proclamation of the Central Committee, published together with the Letter, shows up its attempts to evade basic discussions:

We do not shrink from self-criticism, nor from that of the working class, because we are of their flesh and blood. We declare clearly and plainly: it is not a matter of individuals, but of the Party and revolution, when we ourselves, under the leadership of the Comintern, undertake to correct deviations from the Bolshevik line.

The Communist Party does not turn to the Right, but towards Bolshevism, alongside which there can be no 'more Left' policy except one consisting of empty phraseology.

Ernst judged the situation by its objective political appearance, undervaluing the so-called 'personal factor', the fears, ambitions, vanity, which hampered the work of consolidation at every step. He wrote to me in September 1925: 'The Party discussions are so far very unedifying and unpolitical. In the provinces they have instigated an unheard of slanderous campaign against me. But those are the last efforts. I am and remain optimistic even if not as far as the immediate future is concerned.'

I was far more uneasy. I happened to be in Russia soon after the appearance of the Letter, and had first hand information of Zinoviev's report and general mood. For Russian consumption, a good formula was found: an excellent Left party had been led astray by irresponsible intellectuals; it became necessary to put them in their place. Thaelmann, who represented 'the proletarian element', had only been a victim of cunning and deception. But now he had thrown off the bondage of the intellectuals and emerged as the man he really was – the true leader of German Communism.

The Zinoviev letter seemed to be doing its work. Ernst was brought into the Politbureau, and, under the guidance of the Centre, the long-neglected United Front tactics came to life again and brought immediate results. The most spectacular of these was the successful campaign against meeting the demands of the Kaiser's family for three thousand million marks compensation. The campaign first met with stout opposition from the SPD, but the Communist-led drive found a wide response among workers and a great number of ruined and non-compensated middle-class people. The vigour of popular feeling compelled the SPD to sanction the movement and collaborate with the Communists.

The Party was recovering and people were inclined to ignore the heavy whip of the Comintern looming over them. In March 1926, Ernst was summoned to Moscow to take part in the

Sixth Plenum of the Comintern Executive. His first impressions were described in a letter of 15 March:

> . . . You cannot conceive what a thick wall of mistrust there is to be broken through. In yesterday's debates I was no longer pictured as Hannibal outside or inside the gates, but as a ravenous wolf out to devour Teddy [Thaelmann] skin and bones. On the other side, Gregor [Zinoviev] explicitly stated that my taxation programme and the programme dealing with the Dawes Plan were completely correct and that Teddy and Ruth were in the wrong!

Now, could you wish for more? I told him that his words would have been of consequence had they been spoken one and a half years sooner and in public – to which he said nothing.

In another letter Ernst wrote:

> They postponed the discussions of German affairs until my arrival. Gregor at once talked to me for half-an-hour and asked for another meeting after his lecture. Manuilsky and several others asked me to refrain from attacks. They expect, i.e. fear, that I am going to dish out some beatings . . . Lozovsky invited me for tomorrow. I have not seen Jaglom yet. Atmosphere dull.

In spite of the journey, I feel quite well and already have reasons for optimism.

Teddy was pleasant like a bear.

The Comintern could do no wrong. If Ernst had to be readmitted to the top leadership, he must, of necessity, have undergone a change of heart and turned to the Left. Otherwise, it would mean that the German Central Committee had turned to the Right !

Who approached whom played a great part in the Sixth Plenum debates. Zinoviev and Bukharin set out to convince the conference that Ernst did all the approaching. Then came Stalin who crowned the debates with an argument of his own. He followed, he said, 'the clever speech of Comrade Ernst Meyer with interest'; however, he found it impossible to agree with him on one point. Ernst Meyer claims that the Comintern adopted his policy, but, 'Ernst Meyer is known to be an advocate of the Right. The Central Committee of the German Communist Party cannot adopt the Right's view without turning back the wheel of Communist history. It follows then that Ernst Meyer changed his views and approached the Central Committee'.

For good measure, he gave Ernst a fatherly admonition to make 'two or three steps' forward and to discard more of his errors. Ernst mocked that he was all in favour of 'making steps', and repeatedly asked what his errors were. But no one ventured an answer.

Ruth Fischer was accused of many things: sluggishness in fighting the ultra-left, neglect of trade union work, 'insufferable' treatment of Social-Democratic workers and, counting very highly with the Bolshevik Party, lack of collective work within the Central Committee. But all this had not determined her fall. Zinoviev was very careful in his conclusions, neither recommending nor even considering her removal from the leadership.

But she was the most outstanding figure of the Left and too ambitious for the Russians. Thaelmann was much better suited to the role of puppet. In a private talk with Ernst, he said he would surround himself with a set of secretaries, including Ernst, to work for him. 'The policy will come from Moscow anyhow', he concluded wisely. Thus power was handed over to the Thaelmann-Dengel group which was distinguished from the outgoing leadership in nothing but lack of talent and ideas. They all worked in perfect unison and were first to introduce that perilous uniformity chiefly responsible for the disintegration of Communism throughout the world. It soon became obvious that Thaelmann's position was much stronger than could be expected and he had a free hand in further manoeuvring it to his advantage.

The split caused by the Open Letter was on the whole negligible. The majority of Ruth Fischer's initial supporters soon jumped on the bandwagon and were allowed to keep their positions. The Left leadership thus remained intact, retaining its former 'reliable' staff and in no hurry to reinstate those forces capable of affecting changes. Although the policy of the *Centre Group* was accepted it was unashamedly referred to as the 'Right', and talk of Right danger went on unchanged. The term 'ultra-left' which marked former policy was carefully omitted. It was, to all intents and purposes, much safer to have belonged to the discarded Left. The Comintern thus set the Party the insoluble task of fighting ultra-left policy while upholding its champions and lashing out at their critics, the 'Right'.

These off-hand frivolous dealings with the German crisis were often attributed to the mounting nationalism of the Russian Party caused by Stalin's 'Socialism in One Country'. But this does not explain how Trotsky himself, the internationalist par excellence, also underestimated the calamity and, most decidedly, the sorry part Zinoviev played in it. At a meeting with Ernst in March, 1926, Trotsky asked him: 'What do the German workers think of Zinoviev?'

'I am convinced that if Lenin were alive he would have him hanged for the harm he has done to the German movement. Yes, I mean what I say: physically destroyed.'

'Is it your private opinion or that of the German workers?'

'I am their representative and hope to express correctly their thought and feeling.'

'I think you are exaggerating, Comrade Meyer.'

'As you wish, Comrade Trotsky.'

Ernst's answer was obviously an expression of his bitterness, but it nevertheless conveyed his true opinion of Zinoviev. He wrote to me in August 1926: 'My wrath against the wreckers is strong but no less than that against all their sponsors of the last two and a half years. We are facing the most serious crisis since Heidelberg. We may not suffer any severe losses but our isolation will increase temporarily. The Central Committee is still unable to gather strength for a vigorous policy and shows no insight in dealing with future perspectives.'

Ernst tried for quite a while to guess why Trotsky was so annoyed – the secret of his forthcoming merger with Zinoviev was well kept. He obviously needed the illusion of Zinoviev's importance, and chose not to assess his role properly. The new tasks of the Russian leaders demanded all their efforts and did not leave much room for thorough investigation of international problems. They, above all, obscured understanding and judgement of essentially pre-revolutionary tactics – to them a matter of the past. On 18 August 1926, Ernst wrote:

I had a detailed discussion with Bukharin . . . In contrast to March, he was very amiable, agreed with me on all political questions and asked only for patience. He was even more critical than I towards Teddy and the Central Committee . . . He spoke disparagingly of Heinz N. (Neumann) and even of Teddy. But over there they are still lacking the courage to break with or even to upbraid him. They are afraid he might make yet another somersault and therefore continue to make personal concessions to him . . . Bukharin does not harbour the faintest illusions about him or his group.

Ernst knew he was in for a long struggle and was terrified at the deterioration of the Russian section of the Comintern. He told Bukharin: 'For the first time I am leaving Russia with the growing feeling that there is nothing I can learn from her leaders.'

11.

Russia, 1925

Journeying to Leningrad by boat, I could immediately feel the great changes. It was 1925, the happiest time in Soviet history, and I felt transplanted into another world. It was not the world of austerity and the grim struggle for survival I saw in 1922.

On board were some NEP-men – grown rich through the workings of the New Economic Policy – and they were allowed to travel and indulge in Western luxuries on the firmly stabilised Soviet rouble. Everybody seemed moved by a spirit of great hope and unlimited expectation which lent them a vigour and liveliness long extinguished in the Germany I left behind me. Here on the boat the children of the NEP-men were allowed to take part in the activities of the Communist youngsters and they sang the new stirring songs with the same enthusiasm.

Leningrad's harbour, with endless formalities and bureaucratic muddle, was annoying. I missed my prospective hostess and was left to fend for myself. I felt quite lonely for a moment, but was immediately at home when I entered the tram. It was packed with people, clean, well fed, simply but adequately clad, engrossed in their evening papers. They were not looking for gossip or sport; this could easily be gauged because the Russian papers carry their political columns on the first page. We had the same interest, we read the same papers, it was like belonging to a large family. This feeling was intensified every minute, enhanced by the sight of unusual processions passing by. Russia was celebrating the bi-centenary of the Academy of Science. Hundreds of men and women were marching with red flags, and the passengers became animated: 'Our people are going to the station to see the foreign scientists off to Moscow. Quite a number of visitors have arrived. Let them see our achievements.' The backward Russian workers honouring the Academy of Science! Where else could such a demonstration take place!

The words 'we', 'us', 'ours', could be heard everywhere – 'our bus', 'have you seen our new buildings?', 'our gardens', 'our nurseries' – by far not many, by far not enough, but 'ours'.

I went to see the Peter-Paul fortress on the Neva river which had served both as a mausoleum for the dead Tsars and a prison for revolutionaries and other adversaries of the state. A popular saying defined it as a place 'where they carry dead Tsars in and dead revolutionaries out'. Very few escaped the place alive. It also contained a special wing for enemies of the Tsars from their own close circles: courtiers and other dignitaries. Their identity was kept secret even from the jailors.

With enough imagination one might be able to conceive what life in a fortress meant. But one aspect of such martyrdom is beyond human perception: silence. And it was mainly the gruesome silence which caused a great amount of insanity and suicide. We experienced it for a brief moment. Our guide suddenly interrupted his lecture: 'And now comrades, shut your eyes.' He closed the heavy door of the cell. Silence descended from the damp, thick walls, from the ceiling, from everywhere, menacing, gripping us. In a few minutes we grew numb. I was probably the first to open my eyes. The young faces were as white as sheets, looking like corpses in the dimly-lit stone cave. Fists were clenched, ready to take revenge on an invisible enemy.

The Winter Palace, the residence of the Tsars, stood in all

its magnificence just opposite the fortress. Its large windows offered a perfect view of the macabre place. The Tsars did not seem to
have been very sensitive. Or did it add to their feeling of security to
see their adversaries so well entombed?

The Palace had been turned into a revolutionary museum.
History of oppression and revolutionary struggle was shown in pic-
tures and documents, in texts of slave traffic, pictures of weird tor-
ture instruments, of executions and of revolutionaries themselves.
It told of events and personalities from the rebels Stenka Razin and
Pugatchov to our own days.

A letter drew great attention and caused some laughter.
A mother, who had the misfortune to engage Lenin's elder
brother to prepare her boy for secondary school, was pleading for
mercy. Lenin's brother was later executed for revolutionary activities. She assured the Tsar that she and her son knew nothing of the
ideas of the tutor. She happened to be a cook, and the thought that
her son should receive a secondary education was more than the
Tsar could stand. He was so enraged that he wrote in the margin:
'This is just the trouble! A cook sends her children to a secondary
school!'

The visitors, school children, soldiers, workers, were so different from the sightseers of other countries. For instance, they
wanted to know 'in which armchair the Tsar signed death sentences and from which window had he watched the massacre of the
workers in January 1905?'

People looked free and self-confident, they became articulate. The changed social relations could be best observed in holiday
resorts where people confronted each other on a common
ground – in search of health and recreation.

The beautiful Crimean coast was clustered with mansions
and palaces which had been turned into sanatoriums for workers
and peasants. Their inmates were clad in dull uniforms – objects of
much dissension. The revolutionaries, quite a number of whom
spent many years in Tsarist prisons, complained that the clothes
reminded them of their gloomy past.

Side by side stood private sanatoriums for the high paid

scientists, specialists – and the 'new rich'. 'New' should not be confused with the current notion of war-time profiteers and other easily enriched people, looked down upon by well-to-do educated society. They mostly belonged to the same well-established circles of
the old rich, who had lately been allowed private enterprise again.
They looked well cared for, well turned out, they had furs, jewellery.
But, oh, they seemed embarrassingly out of place and, to a degree,
even pitiful. It positively required courage to belong to that set. It
was not the smart dresses and jewels which had given distinction to
the possessing classes, but their feeling of security in a dominant position. This they now had lost. Our ugly, uniform outfits were as
awe-inspiring as diamonds and tiaras – they were a sign of 'belonging'.

You made another discovery: manners, 'good manners'
were in no way a matter of aesthetic refinement. Here they had
changed within one decade. To be called 'lady' was nearly an insult,
to be called Comrade, a distinction comparable only with Sir or
Lord. Handkissing, all the codes of good behaviour established by
the upper classes simply disappeared. (Characteristically, they
came to the fore again in 1928, when the government got into difficulties.) The upper circles were trying to borrow manners, behav-
ior and even the language of those who were succeeding them.

Of course, there were quite a few go-getters, scheming,
grabbing careerists, exploiting the new opportunities for their own
ends only. Yet they differed from their counterparts in other countries. They too were touched by the new requirements, if not mood.
Their progress closely depended on the prosperity of the new state
and they were ready to make their contributions, going even so far
as to concern themselves with world affairs.

Passing through villages with decrepit huts, impassable
roads, filthy urchins in rags, or dwellings secluded by high walls,
where the native Tartars still kept their womenfolk in fear and slav-
ery, a vision of what lay ahead of the new crusaders flashed through
my mind. How would they overcome so much poverty, superstition
and darkness? My Russian friends seemed undaunted: 'Oh, yes, we
know. But we have started.'

The women presented a great paradox. They were given all the rights and advantages of equality and opportunity, but they lost the security of a home and a man just for themselves, 'for better or for worse'. And they looked forlorn and bewildered. Easy divorces were a one-sided matter: 'You need two to live in harmony but only one to separate.' In the early stages of the Revolution the most trifling squabbles led to divorce, although this did not lead to moral dissipation. Contrary to the spicy gossip columns of the anti-Bolshevik press, promiscuity was rare in the early years of the Revolution – Radek explained this as another proof of its stability and wholesomeness. In fact people were too absorbed in the new tasks to have much time for what was called 'personal life'. Cold and hunger did not predispose one to it either. 'Romantic talk is now reduced to: 'what have you got this week on your ration card?', reported a very attractive woman, who managed to fall in love and marry despite all the sobering circumstances.

The men appeared to be the main beneficiaries of the loosened divorce and marriage regulations and they played havoc with their women. In bourgeois society they, as a rule, chose easy prey among other classes and treated their own girls with more care – no such consideration could be observed here. Abortions, practised on an intolerably high scale, were ruinous to mind and health. I heard many stories of resignation and disillusionment. The atmosphere was so different from the easy comradely one I was accustomed to in my early youth. A passionate walker, I found to my distress that it was rather dangerous to invite a man for company, this was usually met with ambiguous remarks and smiles from fellow guests, men and women alike, and it required elaborate persuasion to make it clear that a walk meant that and nothing more. Endless allusions to 'moon bathing' in ingenious variations formed the general table talk.

To my surprise, no allowance for equality was made in sexual matters. The idea that a girl loses in esteem and value if easily accessible was in full strength. The same jokes, the same attitude towards women still prevailed in the sanatoriums I visited in 1931 and even 1933.

This by no means implies that 'eternal love' vanished from revolutionary Russia. There was enough of it and of sufficient complexity to fill volumes of good old-fashioned novels.

The Soviet government had assigned me a life-pension as Leviné's widow, but only half the money was paid out. My marriage, according to Soviet laws, made no difference and it did not afford me financial security in any case. I did not claim the rest when I was able to earn a living, but my health was now disturbing – it was the beginning of my tuberculosis – and so was Ernst's shaky political position over the past two years. I felt I had no right to expose Leviné's son to my own unstable destinies and decided to ask for restoration of his part of the allowance. Zinoviev was familiar with the case and could help me.

I was also hoping to ask him how he could, with his clear vision of German affairs, allow matters to drag on for so long with no hint of open disapproval. I promised to be very careful and Ernst liked the idea: 'I am convinced you will sugar the pill so well that he will swallow it without noticing.' On arrival in Moscow I rang up Zinoviev's secretariat and asked for an appointment. I gave my name and explained that I was stopping in Moscow only for a few days. I had to ring again and again, and was finally told: 'Comrade Zinoviev is just recovering from an illness which kept him away from office, and is overwhelmed with work. He will hardly be able to see you.'

'Does Zinoviev know of my request?'

'No. I am trying to disturb him as little as possible.'

'I will accept a refusal from none but Zinoviev himself.'

'What was your name?'

I told him. No, he did not know. I snapped: 'Not quite commendable for a secretary of Comrade Zinoviev.' He went to announce me at once and was very apologetic on his return: 'Comrade Zinoviev asked me to tell you that he will definitely see you. I shall let you know the moment he is free.' He went on apologising: 'Of course, I know the name of Meyer and Levine'. It was the combination of the two names which confused me.'

I was far from insinuating that a man of Zinoviev's responsibilities should always be available to visitors, but the contrast between the former cold indifference of the secretary and his later servility indicated an attitude in high places which was highly disturbing. The incident went round among my Russian friends and there was great indignation about 'the deterioration of Zinoviev's entourage'. Was criticism so severe only because Zinoviev was 'slipping'? His loss of prestige in the German party was unknown here. He had managed to make his 'Open Letter' look like a parental reminder to children who overstepped the line. It did not amount to much: 'it was necessary to push aside the intellectuals, Ruth Fischer and Maslow, and give the true proletarian section of the Central Committee more scope. And it was unpardonable the way these people treated the old cadres, quite incompatible with Bolshevik traditions.'

My friends did not go too deeply into German affairs. As long as the main object, the revolution, was not imminent, they were prepared to accept anything. Even the few better informed were not too hard on Zinoviev and did not expect him to fall. The inner struggle had not yet come to a head, he was still the mighty ruler of Leningrad.

People were only extremely sensitive in matters of uncomradely behaviour and were delighted that I put the secretary in his place. Three more days passed and I had not yet achieved my purpose. I did not trust the secretary. I rang up and told him firmly: 'I am not interested in good intentions. If I am to see Zinoviev it must be now.' It worked again: 'Could you come at once?' I went through many gates and doors, being cautioned: 'He is very busy.' It was not necessary. I felt discouraged and gave up all hope of a friendly conversation.

Three years had passed since I last saw Zinoviev. He had grown flabbier, heavier, and seemed a part of the massive chair, which he left for a moment in order to welcome me. His face was colourless, his eyes dull, almost unseeing behind half-closed lids.

The dimly lit room added a sombre touch to his figure and to the whole setting.

'Like Ivan the Terrible! He is dead, a corpse sitting on a throne!' These words were flashing through my mind in steady repetition and haunted me for a long time.

He received me cordially, and I submitted the request to restore my son's pension. I could not refrain from rubbing in: 'to secure him from the unsteady fortunes of his step-father, Ernst Meyer'.

He remembered the case well. They had made a mistake. He made a note, he would see to it. But my allusion to 'unsteady fortunes' worked: 'How is your husband? How is his health?'

I allowed myself another little provocation: 'It was naturally very affected by sad Party affairs.'

He fell for it and began a strangely incoherent monologue about forthcoming changes. He spoke in the casual manner of a great emperor with gracious concern for the destinies of an impoverished vassal or the way one discussed the incompetence of domestic servants.

'Ernst Meyer is still a member of the Prussian Diet as he was before?'

This made me forget all my diplomatic restraint. I stamped my foot and shouted: 'He is not and you know it.'

He knew indeed. The case was sufficiently discussed in the Comintern as it was a particularly ugly affair and an affront to all Party regulations. Becoming quite human for a moment he said helplessly: 'I cannot recollect.' It was pitiful and I left quickly.

I ran out of the Kremlin in a state of terror. Zinoviev had behaved stupidly, downright ludicrously. He would not like me to tell Ernst of our conversation. Still under the spell of the Kremlin atmosphere, I concluded: he will have me kidnapped and incarcerated, or simply destroyed. For the first time I, a faithful, ardent Communist, conceived in a flash the implications of a totalitarian state. So I must not talk, not as long as I am in Russia. Anything could happen. And this was in 1925 . . .

I visited Radek. He was one of the few on whom power left no trace, remaining the same matey, informal man I knew before. But all was not right in his household. He had vowed never to break up his marriage. But the brakes he used to put on deliberately in relationships with other women did not work this time. Larissa Reissner proved too strong. She was young, very attractive, highly talented and ambitious. She was married to Raskolnikov, the Ambassador to Persia and one of the most attractive figures of the Russian Revolution, but abruptly deserted him when his star went on the decline and he lost his post. Rumour had it that she took Radek on the rebound – her real target being the inaccessible Trotsky.

Radek made one concession; he did not 'leave' his wife, nor their common home. But it did not help. Not by the look of his wife. The proud, beautiful woman I had known only three short years before seemed, with her tightly pressed unsmiling lips and empty eyes, drained of all life.

Yet new love, which is supposed to be a great stimulant, failed in Radek's case. I found him very subdued and lacking his former brilliance. My visit coincided with the collapse of Ruth Fischer's reign. He somehow felt obliged to discuss it with me, though he never tried to find out the mood in Germany, or the opinion of Ernst. This was also a monologue – listening was never one of Radek's talents. I found, with great surprise, his views full of easily detectable contradictions and inaccuracies.

The fight against Trotsky was then, in September 1925, at its peak. To remove him from politics and submerge him in routine work, he was given quite a few offices. He was Chairman of the Concession Committee, Head of the Electro-Technical Board and Chairman of the Scientific-Technical Board of Industry. Radek told me, very animatedly, how Trotsky's genius made itself felt wherever he was put to work. Noticing my shoes, he said: 'I must take you to Trotsky. He would examine every stitch, endlessly pump you, and then know how to produce such beauties himself, or even nicer ones.'

As usual he had an anecdote to tell. In one of his articles, he wryly compared the idea of peaceful development of socialism with

bloodless removal of corns. A German product had done this beneficial trick for him. His article appeared under the headline 'Kukirol'
and seemed to have done a lot to boost the firm's business. They con-
scientiously offered him a share of the profits and an appropriate re-
ward for any further services.

Radek was also inundated with offers to write for the Amer-
ican press, on any subject, at any time and at a minimum of $500 a
piece. Not for nothing was he considered the greatest journalist of
his time, but he was not tempted. Revolutionaries did not work
for the bourgeois press.

He had no idea of the pending battle which was to destroy
his life-work and himself.

I stayed in Moscow with the Jagloms and had a good insight
into the life of a high soviet functionary for the first time. On the
face of it, their life corresponded to Lenin's scheme of reducing the
living standards of the highest dignitaries to those of skilled workers. Yet they towered high above ordinary Russian citizens. Jaglom
had no need to spend exhausting hours in crowded vehicles to reach
his various destinations. The family had access to exclusive resting
homes and to treatment in the Kremlin hospital – a good equiva-
lent to the best ones of capitalist countries – to theatre and to other
amenities. Everything was in fact accessible to the Jagloms. This
modest family became a centre of flattering attention. To be sure,
modest only in origin, as they were second to none in talent and human qualities. But their society was sought after far beyond their
personal merits. It must be emphasised that one could hardly find
people less affected by their powerful situation. But it was a dangerous position and it was almost entirely left to the discretion of the
individual how to use it. The workers, the class-conscious, advanced
ones, looked at the problem with resigned tranquillity: 'We must
provide our leading cadres with the best we have. We need them.
They atone for it by inhuman work.'

Later, in 1932, on a long journey between Moscow and
Kiev I met with a crass example of the self-restraint of the workers.
I had a heart-to-heart, truly Russian talk with a worker who was not

a Party member, though he was a staunch Bolshevik supporter from the start. He smiled apologetically: 'I am not fit for the Party – too much of an individualist.' At first he was extremely reserved, repeating the obligatory phraseology about 'our achievements'. I was not getting anywhere, so I took out my papers and let him see my 'credentials'. He studied them carefully and the ice was broken. Suddenly nothing was fine, a picture of hardship and suffering emerged in all its details. As for himself, he did not mind cold, meagre food rations or other privations; he suffered most from being condemned to share a crowded room for years on end..He was longing for privacy: 'Just to shut the door behind me for a short while and be alone in a room. You would not believe what an obsession it can become.'

I was overcome with compassion and mentioned the four tiny rooms allotted to my friend Pankratova, her mother and little daughter. He immediately asked what her job was.

'A scientist?', he said. 'In that case it is not an inch too large. She has to work in peace, to receive people, to keep manuscripts in order. We need our scientists.'

1925 was the most inspiring stage of the Soviets' existence. It seemed that nothing could stop the boom. Hopes ran sky-high. A whole people got up in arms to fight for a 'better world' with skill and originality. Who ever heard of 'Living Newspapers', with events presented in action? Or 'Mural Papers', obligatory for every factory, office, school, for everybody to express their opinion, introduce new ideas, *criticise*?

They carried enlightenment into the Red Army where four hours were designated daily for political and general instruction. And the Red Army in their turn helped to carry out educational tasks in the provinces and remote villages after demobilisation or on leave. I heard a foreign visitor say that their summer camps resembled cultural centres. This was the period when the government had enough self-confidence to entrust the workers with carrying and using firearms. The Army itself was accordingly reduced from five million to a mere 600,000.

And the network of theatres, spreading all over the country, the clubs and recreation centres! The theatres! Meyerhold, from whom our great Max Reinhardt could borrow many a new idea! And all in the teeth of poverty and distraction and the sabotaging by a great part of the intellectual forces. Actors even refused to play for an audience of workers or, what is difficult to understand, levelled down their artistic standards, introduced that carelessness and vulgarity, which the Russians call 'Chaltura'. I saw many plays that were mostly poor, where virtue was invariably rewarded and vice punished. I reasoned: it might look like propaganda but in this country it is sheer unvarnished truth. How could all those miracles happen without the triumph of the good?

One play was a kind of spy thriller, where the revolutionaries penetrated into high society and performed feats of bravery. There was no happy ending. The beautiful heroine – so touching in her sincerity – and her equally attractive accomplices were discovered and led away to torture – and death? There is now one country where crusaders will never be persecuted, I told myself.

Walking on the shockingly paved, feet-wrecking Moscow streets, was like flying in the air. Crowded, smelly, unhygienic dwellings, my greatest torment under any circumstances, discomfort and lack of many things, which became a matter of daily routine, counted for nothing.

12.

Ernst Meyer's Declaration

In December 1926, a session of the Comintern Executive was called to assess the effects of Zinoviev's Open Letter and to decide on the Party's future course. Representatives of the diverse factions had been summoned to Moscow and Ernst's friends were urging him to join the delegation. It was also the wish of the Central Committee. But it was not an order, he could refuse to go, if he so desired. Everything seemed to favour the journey. It was advantageous to attend the discussions, and the pre-Christmas period could always be regarded as a kind of political recess. He also needed money badly and in Moscow could make deals for some of his writings.

From my bed in a Swiss sanatorium, I wrote: 'I don't really know what I want you to do, go to Russia or come here to finish your book . . . They are extremely cautious, will wriggle and certainly not make any decisive changes in German affairs. You will only torment yourself – what for ? Your book is needed more than ever. Really, believe me, it is more important.'

Ernst decided to go after all. It was to be a short session, and in the middle of December I received a telegram: 'Leaving tomorrow. Will be with you for Christmas.' It was followed by another cancelling the first. Then a third with another date, then another. It couldn't be helped. A drama was played out in Moscow which broke

Ernst's spirit and largely contributed to his later illness and death. My judgement had proved correct – the Russians were not in the mood to change their German policy. Thaelmann was to figure as head of the Party. Some of the delegates were frightened into submission, others were excommunicated. Everything was fixed, including Ernst's role. The strong faction had to be split and the best way was an official declaration from Ernst to fight part of it. He was altogether too independent and, along with a strong faction of old experienced leaders, which included many Brandlerites, could become a menace to the Comintern's claim for absolute supremacy. He had to be checked in time, and this was certainly the work of Stalin himself.

At the Sixth Plenum of the ECCI in March 1926, Ernst had fought tooth and nail against the system of demanding declarations. In man to man talks, an agreement was reached to abolish such demands once and for all. This was now changed and Ernst demanded: 'I wish to know what happened to justify the reversal of our former decisions?' Stalin himself undertook to handle the case. He started a long roundabout discourse. Ernst said: 'I'm not listening. I demand clear, political reasons.'

The Comintern by then had stopped bothering much about explanations. But they were very careful not to overdo it. Ernst was not asked to 'admit mistakes' or do other penance, in fact was not asked to say anything contrary to his own policy. Paradoxically, this made his position more difficult. He could not break with the Comintern on what seemed formal grounds. His refusal would at least involve a long struggle with an indefinite stay in Moscow when he was needed in Germany to put into practice a policy which he himself championed. The absurdity of the demands was so flagrant that for a while he was convinced their chief object was his personal humiliation: 'They could not forgive me my firm stand against the ultra-left course while they themselves were so deeply compromised'. It was the first time I heard him apply a personal interpretation to Party policy.

Ernst gave in but he fought hard to secure unequivocal formulation of his own points. Four drafts of a declaration were presented. The first one by Ernst was a bitter attack on extorting declarations and a lesson in Party loyalty and discipline. It was carefully expurgated but the final document still contained a clause stating that his dissociation from the Right wing and his fight against all deviations was only *a continuation* of a policy which *he had always* pursued without any demands of the Comintern. Here is Ernst Meyer's draft of the declaration:

The declarations repeatedly demanded of me in the last 15 months have not succeeded in establishing the cooperation which is needed in the interest of the Party. On the other hand my political conduct during this period proves more than any formal declaration ever could. However, to banish all doubts of my readiness for unreserved collaboration on the political basis of the present Central Committee, I state:

1) Just as I acknowledged the resolutions at the VIth plenary session of the Executive of the Comintern and, as far as the Party accepted my collaboration, and put them into effect, I acknowledge the resolutions of the VIIth session, with which I am in full agreement.

2) I explicitly extend this complete agreement to the decision concerning Comrades Brandler and Thalheimer. I had already openly criticised the political errors of the Central Committee in October 1923, and repeatedly did so, without any exhortations: (Frankfurt Party Conference 1924, Berlin Party Conference 1925, and so on). I shall also in future fight openly against Party members, individuals or groups in the future should they defend or repeat the same or similar mistakes.

I emphatically reject the interpretation that the demands which had been made since March to rescind the prohibition of both comrades from participating in Comintern affairs and their admission to Party work in Germany, in themselves imply concealment or support of their errors. (Comrade Thaelmann also fundamentally agreed to their readmission last March and only wanted to postpone it for tactical reasons.)

Both demands were based on the assumption that this was the best means to combat ideologically the very real deviations of these comrades.

3) My conduct proves that I stand not only verbally but in actual fact on the platform of the Comintern. This statement is necessary in the interest of ideological clarification within the German Communist Party and complete overcoming of ultra-left views among its members.

4) My activities prove more than any declaration that I supported the Central Committee unreservedly if not uncritically. Neither shall I in future make conditions for any kind of collaboration.

5) I have never demanded the incorporation of the Central Committee into my Group; instead I am striving for a complete fusion on the political basis of the present Central Committee.

6) After the dissolution of my group, I for my part, always used my influence to combat hangovers of factional disputes. I shall also contribute all I can in future to this purpose.

7) I shall observe the obligation of party discipline towards any body to which I belong or shall belong.

8) The Party must resolutely and immediately combat all tendencies towards opportunistic deviation and point out these errors by means of concrete examples. I regard this as one of the most essential tasks and shall be in the front line of this struggle.

Moscow, 24 December 1926, Ernst Meyer.

The fourth and final version:

Comrade Meyer declares:

1) He unconditionally and unreservedly accepts the decisions of the 7th plenary session of the Executive and accepts the obligation to work actively for their realisation.

2) In accordance with his agreement with the resolutions of the Seventh Plenary session of the Executive, including the problem of Brandler and Thalheimer, he condemns – just as he has repeatedly done since October 1923–the political errors of these comrades and pledges himself to combat these and similar errors in cooperation with the Central Committee.

3) He unreservedly and unconditionally submits to the leadership of the Central Committee of the Party and its leading organisations and pledges himself to fight together with the Central Committee against both Right as well as ultra-left tendencies. This does not preclude him from exercising criticism within the leading bodies of the Party.

4) Comrade Meyer is obliged to fight together with the Central Committee against any factional activities and groupings within the Party.

5) Comrade Meyer will ensure that his activities both before and at the Party Congress are consistent with the above four points.

If these points are accepted the Central Committee will accord Comrade Meyer full guarantee that he will be permitted to work together with the Central Committee of the Party before, during and after the Congress.

Moscow, 24 December 1926

Signed: Ernst Thaelmann

Signed: Ernst Meyer

There was, however, a point in his declaration which could not be smoothed over: 'He unreservedly and unconditionally submits to the leadership of the Central Committee of the Party and its leading organisations . . .' Not even the Russian leaders had much regard for the existing German staff. Zinoviev admitted that Thaelmann was wrong (as far as he could be credited at all with an independent policy on the main issues of the recent period). It was a flagrant mockery to demand of Ernst submission to a leadership they spoke of so disparagingly. It was a flagrant humiliation to accept it, a surrender of moral integrity. Ernst returned from Moscow a sick man. My doctor looked at him with apprehension: 'I would not know who is the patient in this room, you or your wife.'

The declaration caused a storm among the Brandlerite Section of Ernst's group. They took his promise to fight the Right as a personal affront, which, in a way, it was. But he had formed his faction in the belief that the best way to shed errors was through one's further activities. Lenin had done just this with many Bolshevik leaders, like Zinoviev and Kamenev, drawing them into Party work and making use of their talents. Ernst demanded the same treatment for Brandler and his supporters. Thrashing out problems in the open was the only way of training the Party for future tasks. He never stopped campaigning for the return of Brandler and Thalheimer, ignoring the whispering and at times very noisy accusations that he was thereby exposing his own hidden Rightist inclinations.

Ernst's new group was indispensible as opposition. Yet after they had accepted, even with reservations, the resolutions of the Comintern, they made themselves prisoners to it and the whims of its incompetent emissaries. Of course, no one, not even the Communists' adversaries could foresee the following rapid degeneration of the Comintern. Ernst was aware of Stalin's intention to provoke a split but he expected more rational behaviour from his group. The first meeting with his collaborators was not very promising. His letters of that period mirror all his torment, doubts, bitterness and despair, with only very occasional flashes of confidence and relief:

Berlin, 6 January 1927

. . . In spite of your two letters political affairs keep me in a very bad mood. Therefore I cannot write very well. Depression during the day, confused dreams during the night.

Against me are: Jakob (Walcher), Paul (Froelich), Rosi (Wolfstein), Enderle and with reservations many of the less important.

For me: Gerhart (Eisler), Georg Schumann, Becker, Frank, etc. The first group had a chance majority.

The Central Committee is pursuing a more serious course towards consolidation.

How the entire case will end – peacefully or not – is now difficult to assess.

I am not smoking much, but still don't feel like eating and am in a state of intensified nervousness and go to bed early. When next week's conference is over the tension might lessen.

Your letters are the only comfort.

Berlin, 7 January 1927

You seem to be more affected by my political worries than I. This is quite wrong. I am more and more convinced – especially through the arguments of my friends who defend their dissension – that I was right. Besides, I have already more or less certainly achieved a majority.

But it requires difficult and dangerous manoeuvering. One half of me is lamenting it; the other is attracted by the increased danger.

I have not the slightest doubt that we shall win through in the end.

Berlin, 9 January 1927

Sunday has been lost through a Party session . . . The week has been filled with reports, negotiations with the Central Committee and efforts to keep the majority of our friends intact. If one thinks it possible to win over the majority of the Party, one should naturally be capable of gaining a majority within one's own circle. And this has been achieved. Now I am aiming to unite them *all* on my platform. The prospects for it are also promising. It takes a lot of work. But I have already won over all the influential and active members. It may also be possible to prevent the splitting up of even a small section, which would only be advantageous to the Neumann people . . .

An unsavoury aspect remains: the inevitable decrease of my polit-

ical popularity among the SPD and non-Party workers.
How to prevent it I don't quite know . . .

Berlin, 10 January 1927

I wanted to write to you as soon as I had got your letter and a very
long Central Committee session prevented me. But your understanding and compassion kept me calm throughout the
day, though not to the end of the session, when the very fact
that it should be left to Dengel to defend me against attacks
of the Left seemed offensive and upset me once again . . .

The only thing which surprised me was about Boettcher whom I
saw yesterday and who is set on stating his disapproval of
my declaration and his regret that I thought this sacrifice
necessary on behalf of Jakob's section at the Conference of
secretaries.

As the others (Heinz Neumann, etc.) will use it as a means of playing us off against each other, it will lead to an open split, for
it would force me to dwell in public on all my reasons for
signing. I am still trying to prevent Boettcher's declaration,
but Jakob seems to be bent on splitting the group.

You are right though: the best and most influential members in Berlin and the provinces do share my views.

I feel quite stimulated, not at all depressed. I regard the adversities
as a spur and challenge.

12 January 1927

I'm gradually succeeding in getting a stronger hold on the reins. Di-
plomacy and threats, yielding and rebukes must be carefully
dosed to direct the Central Committee, the group and the
sympathisers into the appropriate channels. A few
incidents – as is usually the case – helped me. Nevertheless, tomorrow is the Conference of secretaries and the de-
vil only knows what will happen, for you can't rely on anyone despite all agreements.

Lominadse is here again. He supported me today on all issues. But
there are also counter-pressures.

Berlin, 13 January 1927

Afternoon (at the session):

The main coup is over. Paul Boettcher unfortunately made me the target of his attacks rather than the Central Committee. This forced me, in turn, to get involved in a sharp exchange with him even though I spoke in a comradely way. The breach has therefore now taken place. I am sorry to lose Boettcher and Jakob. But it could not be avoided. My speech made a strong impression. 'A ministerial attention' said Frank.

The Central Committee immediately turned it down. Of course, it will continue making difficulties especially in matters of personnel. But it is nevertheless a move forward.

On the other side, I now carry a great share of responsibility for the Central Committee. My friends will hurl each of its misdeeds at me.

The theses of the Central Committee for the Party congress must now be singularly lucid, i.e. I must carefully work them out together with Gerhart, Ludwig and Becker.

My prestige has not suffered in any case, though Boettcher explicitly aimed at it in his attacks. It has even increased. I pointed out, by the way, that I knew better methods of achieving consolidation than demands for public declarations and that I struggled against it. I 'shall nevertheless stick to my declaration'. I must wait and see how it will all turn out. I assume, better than I expected in Moscow . . . I'm also much less tense . . .

14 January 1927

. . . My tension has completely gone. The doubts of the best of my friends will be resolved by my further activity. The rest will be just chaff. Yesterday I used a sentence from one of your letters. To Boettcher's warning that the declaration will impair my authority I said: my political reputation does not depend on one particular act but on all my former activities and my future work. (Spontaneous calls: 'Very true'.) My speech yesterday, on the contrary, enhanced my authority.

23 January 1927

The barriers between me and the rank and file have completely broken down; the last remnants because of my declaration. They don't feel that it was a very exacting demand. Perhaps they will appreciate in future that it was on my part a sacrifice to the Party.

6 February 1927

I am at peace only when I am with you. As soon as I am away all the Party turmoil storms over me. I suffered under the pressure with undiminished intensity and it eased only after the conference. But even now the slightest parallel evokes the torment of December.

To this day I don't reproach myself but it wears me down – to struggle against even those with whom I basically agree, like Jakob and Braun, instead of peacefully collaborating. It is even worse, at least more distressing than during Ruth's time. I am, therefore, also physically very weak, and am often tired.

Yet it was not the split in the group which formed the core of his despair. True, it forced him to dwell more intensely on the errors of the Right than was profitable for the Party, suffering as it was from ultra-left afflictions. But this was a problem of no great immediate consequence. Rather, it was the injury to his integrity which made him write on 15 January:

. . . I have been thinking of the last few weeks. I have become a different person. My hatred is as strong as on the day I signed the declaration. I feel bruised. It is true, the Conference was a success. The declaration was also necessary. The result will, in the end, prove advantageous to the Party. But it remains a sacrifice . . . You are right: it was a choice between forfeiting the right or left eye. But perhaps it would have been better to lose life itself than to accept such a choice. I consider it the worst experience I have ever had in all my activities. It cannot pass without leaving scars for life.

On the eve of the Essen Party Conference, he sent me a passionate love letter:

Bremen, 27 February 1927

Sweetest love!

I drank a bottle of alcohol and some brandy – all on my own and I'm dreaming of you. When you're not there I have a constant need to get drunk or for stimulation. All kinds of ideas are blossoming, quite unknown and beautiful, whose centre is you and you again. The last twelve years of Party work have stifled and inhibited me so much. Now, aware, that my efforts have been in many respects futile, I almost regret my conscientiousness. I think I should rather have enjoyed life with you, travelling, seeing and relishing things with you. The memory of a *single* night with you in Neukoelln, Westend, Eisleben is more vivid, satisfying than all the rest. I am thinking of the time when we shall make up for it and that the April I am to spend in Leysin is so close.

I am waiting in the cafe for my political friends but would much prefer to catch a train and come to you. In such moments I am much nearer to you and your way of thinking. All the longing of youth comes to the surface and also the awareness that it found fulfillment in you and will do so even more in future. In such hours I also know fully why you love me.

Sweetest, only love, I feel so near to you, understand you so well, should like to talk with you, hear of your dreams, listen to your joyful cries and kiss and caress you endlessly. I am not even excited, I have only a strong desire to be with you, to feel you, to listen to you, to see your smooth, fresh, dear face, and to proudly soak in your joy of my presence.

Ernst went to the Essen Party Conference of February 1927, as if going to the slaughter. He was a stranger to the leading body and had no faith in Brandler's associates: 'I don't, of course, let it get the better of me but it is the worst struggle I have ever had to face. Above all it is fraught with greater danger of committing errors than in all former situations. The question is presented this way: a breach with part of the group and *unconditional* merger with the Central Committee; or a complete breach with the Central Committee, which would still not erase the discontent of a part of the group. Jakob will definitely stick to Heinrich Br. and August Th.'

He went through the congress choking in the atmosphere of intrigue, gossip and duplicity. But the familiar routine of a Party rally sometimes carried him away:

Essen, 5 March 1927

I am in good spirits, at least I was until this evening. But Boettcher and Jakob are stirring up feeling against me just as much as Brandler was at Leipzig. One of their foolish mouth-pieces this evening dared to make the insolent criticism that my declarations were in any case sheer hypocrisy. As soon as I say a single political word to parry their attacks they rave about treason. Jakob and Boettcher lost their heads and manoeuvred themselves into complete isolation.

Disregarding all personal considerations, I stand, I believe, successfully, for Boettcher's election into the Central Committee. Perhaps I am *too* fair after all.

Otherwise the Congress is really a success. Every day Social Democratic, non-Party and even workers of the Roman Catholic Centre appear to greet us. Very moving was a delegation of the 'Young Spartacus' in white blouses and with their own orchestra. After many years I am again listening daily with relish to the 'Internationale'.

Klara (Zetkin) is expected. Lominadse told me that she in no way approves of Boettcher's attacks against me.

Everything proceeded according to schedule: Ernst was

again elected as one of the five members of the Politbureau. But distressing letters soon followed:

Berlin, 8 March 1927

Sweet love,

I am back home, tired from the strain of the Congress and my cold which still hasn't subsided yet, and though, in the last analysis, everything took the expected course, I feel disappointed. The attitude of a section of my former friends is harmful to the Party and creates new dangers. It is naturally also no pleasure to be submitted to attacks prompted by their own stupidity.

I have also been elected into the Politbureau and for the time being I keep my post at the press agency.

Oh, darling, I am longing for you as always and particularly now in my Leipzig mood. Though it is a reversed Leipzig it is now the beginning of really fruitful work and influence. Intensified work might bring the satisfaction my position ought to give me.

The alliance with Ernst was formally accepted, the agreement formally signed. But the 'wedding', as it was called at a preliminary conference, turned out a war of attrition. The situation remained as untenable as it was before the Congress. Flattered and acclaimed by the Comintern as the 'historic leadership' the Left had forgotten all about their dismal past. The Centre Group was treated as suspect. It was much safer to have belonged to the 'elite', even if their policy was dismissed and its chief initiators, Ruth Fischer and Maslow, condemned and expelled.

The advice and resolutions of Ernst's section were accepted surreptitiously. His own editorial articles appeared anonymously. There is no need to sign such articles and Ernst would hardly have noticed the omission of his name. But he could not fail to see that there was method in it, when the articles of Thaelmann and other favourites always bore their signatures. But these were innocent pin-pricks compared with the deliberate campaign of the Comintern, which resorted to lies in order to discredit him. Ernst was compelled to write to *Pravda* and to Tass in March 1927:

> Dear Comrades,
>
> I would like you to accept the following corrections. In your reports on the Essen Congress of the Communist Party you call me 'a former adherent of the Brandler-Thalheimer Group' and allege that I stressed, in the interest of solidarity, the necessity of openly admitting former mistakes.
>
> To this I must state: I took a sharp view of Brandler's Central Committee immediately in October 1923 and belonged to the so-called Centre Group which was in no way regarded as opportunistic by the Executive. On the contrary, the Executive demanded that the former Left should build a block with the Centre Group for common leadership.
>
> After the Frankfurt Party Congress (in the spring, 1924), part of the Centre Group joined Ruth Fischer and since then Ruth Fischer has labelled the rest of the Group as 'Brandlerists'. My 'opportunism' consisted, among other things, of demands for resistance to the Dawes Plan and of my attitude to tax problems, both of which were explicitly acknowledged as correct at the VIth Plenary Session of the Executive, and even by Comrade Zinoviev.
>
> At the Congress of the Communist Party in Berlin (July 1925) I submitted, together with a few other comrades a detailed platform in the form of an 'open letter' which no one has, as yet, attempted to criticise as opportunist. This platform has won the support of some members who belonged to the former Brandler Group.
>
> In my declaration of December 1926 I acknowledged the resolutions of the Seventh Session of the Executive which contain not a single word of criticism of my policy.
>
> In my declaration I repeated my readiness to fight against the errors of Brandler and Thalheimer, 'just as I have repeatedly done before'. It does not include any obligation to join afterwards in ultra-left criticism of Brandler and Thalheimer.
>
> In my declaration I acknowledge the leadership of the Central Com-

mittee. It includes, as its prerequisite my right of criticism within the leading bodies. The extent to which I intend to use this right I plainly indicated at the Essen Congress.

My declaration is supplemented by a common agreement where the Central Committee secures me the full guarantee of collaboration.

In view of these facts your comments in the Tass telegram are incomprehensible to me.

He also wrote to the Politbureau:

Leysin, 28 November 1927

Dear Comrades

In his answer to Zinoviev's 21 new conditions, Kuusinen promptly fell for Zinoviev's demagogy concerning the Party leadership.

I remind you that the September Plenum of our Central Committee thoroughly rejected, in the interest of the Party, the methods of playing off members of the leadership against each other.

C.Kuusinen's upholding against me the 'more left', in the past 'less discredited', leaders is in gross contradiction to the decision of the September Plenum.

My promise of loyal collaboration does not allow for a disloyal confrontation with the former policy of the leadership.

His allegation that in my declaration I myself admitted Right errors is only designed to mislead our Party membership. I see nothing disreputable in admitting one's errors. But Comrade Kuusinen knows perfectly well that all he could say to my repeated and persistent questions, which then were my 'Right errors' was: they existed in my 'subconscious'.

You cannot very well fight against such moral evaluations. But to define openly as a 'Rightist' everyone who had not committed ultra-left mistakes, is a concession to the ideology of the Left opposition.

I request the Politbureau to inform Comrade Kuusinen of my letter and to draw his attention to the fact that neither false allegations about individual members of the Politbureau nor the attempt at discrimination between them would serve the interests of the Party and the consolidation of the leadership. A decision to this effect will certainly impel Kuusinen to rectify his allegations.

With comradely greetings
Ernst Meyer

Some months later, he also found it necessary to write to Bukharin:

6 February 1928

Dear Comrade Bukharin,

In your concluding speech at the Fifteenth Party Congress, you alleged that in my declaration I have renounced my former mistakes. Referring to my letter of the 28 November 1927 to the Central Committee of the German Communist Party concerning Kuusinen's similar statement, and the answer of the Central Committee (officially repudiating Kuusinen's allegation), I make the following statement: In my declaration of 24 December 1926 there is not a word about former mistakes. My declaration solely deals with the question of my abstention from *public* criticism at that time in the interest of a well consolidated leadership.

Any other allegations are *untrue*.

I trust that, at the next session of the Executive, this matter will finally be put right.

With comradely greetings
Ernst Meyer

When Ernst visited me in the Leysin sanatorium in April, I noticed that his health was improving, and I was inclined to think he had forgotten the declaration and was looking forward to resuming his work. But a change became apparent almost immediately after we arrived back in Germany. He worked as usual, never missing a day or an hour for that matter. But he was always very tired and listless. He rushed home as before, but he hardly talked and laughter almost vanished from our house. His weekends were usually spent at conferences, mostly out of town. On one particular Saturday afternoon he came home pale and shaky. He had intended to leave that evening for the Sunday conference, but could not make it after all, and decided to take an early train next morning.

It was the beginning of an illness which ended in his early death. His high temperature did not recede and it soon became obvious that it was more than an ordinary cold which could in any case require more than a monthly holiday to restore his health. My own time was up, autumn was approaching and I had to return to Leysin for further treatment. I refused to go unless he promised to accompany me for at least two months. Weil had, in the meantime, inherited his father's fortune and offered to pay our bills.

Ernst suffered unbearable pain in the ribs. No one knew the reason and he himself quietly assumed it was cancer. He bore it stoically, serenely, never uttering a single complaint, never showing any irritation or signs of sickness. He only told me of his 'diagnosis' when it transpired that it was 'only' tuberculosis.

Was it a self-inflicted disease when an 'overburdened mind refused to function and ordered the body to take over'? It seemed so plausible. Did he want to live at all? He had too much faith in the revolution, that is, in the Party, which were inseparable for him. Despite the gaining of 3¼ million votes in the 1928 elections, and a new optimism by some leaders, the Party itself was sick. The unhealthy atmosphere created by upholding the Left and fighting the Right, corrupted the whole organisation. The moral decline inevitably brought a harrowing decline in theoretical standards. There were many schools for 'Marxist-Leninist' study, but abstract theoretical knowledge contrasted with practical application only bred more confusion.

The Party cannot rise above the level of its leaders, and the leadership of the German Party was to all intents and purposes in the hands of Thaelmann and Dengel.

13.

Russia, 1928

I was longing for Russia. I had left it in the autumn of 1925, at the peak of its recovery from war and civil war. Like the Russians themselves I saw before me a long unbroken path of achievements and improvements leading to our ultimate victory. I was burning to breathe again the spirit of pioneering and experiment and forget for a while the stale and uneventful life of the western side of the world. My idea seemed sound; there could be no better place than Russia for a long cure and convalescence, since there was an excellent sanatorium for bone tuberculosis. I also thought that Ernst was altogether too close to German affairs, reports, papers, etc. We left for the Soviet Union in early June of 1928.

Among the many visitors to the USSR at that time was Thaelmann, who came for a private conference. For the first time I had a close look at the man who was entrusted with the destiny of the German revolutionary movement. An embarrassed, pleasant looking man in his late thirties rushed into Ernst's room, not even giving me a simple nod of his head much less the customary German hand-shake. It must have been the atmosphere of our 'intelligentsia' home which confused him so. In spite of his high position, flattery, all the rigmarole of the 'personality cult' surrounding him he remained strictly proletarian throughout his reign – which was perhaps his great personal attraction.

'What a lovable child' I exclaimed. Ernst laughed and said that he was always beguiled by Teddy's manners. 'Teddy', the darling toy bear, was the affectionate nick-name he received from quick-witted Berliners.

Thaelmann was another of the Comintern's casualties. A devoted revolutionary, a good orator with a fine instinct for the workers' temper, he was an excellent medium for expounding theories and ideas laid down by others. He was a poor thinker, and not given to abstract study, even lacking enough self-discipline to reach the cultural and theoretical level of an average Party member.

Neither was he particularly stable as was shown by his quick desertion of Ruth Fischer, and also by his personal habits. He drank, at times somewhat beyond his capacity.

He had cut a very handsome figure as the proletarian show-piece in Ruth Fischer's Central Committee. But to make him the indisputable leader of German Communism was to behead the movement and at the same time transform a highly attractive, able personality into a mere puppet.

The power of propaganda and habit was so effective that even the higher Party ranks ended believing in Thaelmann's myth. Yet, panicked by the imminence of Hitler's ascension to power one of the Russian emissaries ran to Thaelmann for salvation. He told me in stupefaction that he found a desperate and confused man who confessed that he had not the slightest idea what to do or what to say.

Another attraction of the journey for me was the forthcoming first Industrial Trial of a clique of industrial experts who conspired with hostile foreign countries to stem the advance of Russia's development. They committed acts of deliberate mis-planning and breakdowns which caused destruction and even death. They all pleaded guilty. And confessions and self-accusations on such scale as theirs were a novelty which left everybody, friends and foes, in acute bewilderment. The defendants, it was explained, had succumbed to the *moral* pressure of the new socialist society. Another triumph of the new order – why not? So many miraculous things happened – I was satisfied and full of happy anticipation.

The trial was in its early days, and I set out with great zeal to get immediate access to the Hall of Columns where it was taking place. I made sure to be as close as possible to the tribunal so as not to miss a word or gesture of those unique defendants. I was in fact so close that I caused a little disturbance. Krylenko, the Public Prosecutor, spotted the 'foreign element' and stopped the proceedings to investigate. What was he afraid of? It was an open trial.

I listened, watched their faces and spare movements and became apprehensive. People don't act this way, don't look this way. They don't confess to such ugly, unsavoury crimes with the smugness and self-assurance of delivering a well-studied lesson, or with such unhesitating willingness. On the rare occasions when the easy flow of their narrative threatened to falter, there was a witness or two at hand to finish the tale. And this was accompanied by approving nods from the defendants themselves.

During a recess I came across a group of their wives and relatives who seemed strangely unaffected. There was neither anxiety nor undue embarrassment in their behaviour, as if the trial were something unreal, a kind of game.

I returned to our hotel deeply disturbed. 'Something is wrong, Ernst, it does not fit. There is a nightmarish atmosphere about it all.'

'Perhaps the trial was not well prepared politically', he answered.

None of us suspected for one moment the truth of the indictment. But the verdicts startled me anew, they seemed arbitrary, void of any logic. The same indictment, fundamentally the same conditions and extenuating circumstances – yet different punishment, varying between relatively light sentences and firing squads. I suggested a game: picking out some cases, I described their essential features and let Ernst guess the verdict. He was invariably wrong. After I had watched the procedure of the trial I believed I could even find a clue to the confessions. Caught in a net of innumerable witnesses, confrontations with other defendants in whose guilt they might honestly and reciprocally have believed (breakdowns and bad industrial accidents did occur after all) they might have grown weary of a futile struggle and decided to give in. At least, it might secure some leniency.

Yet, had the authorities themselves been taken in by a diabolic plot? For the trial, which deprived the industry of skilled, experienced men and caused confusion and fear all round, was obviously of greater service to the enemies of the Soviet state.

Ernst was received very cordially in Moscow, and Bukharin was extremely friendly and helpful. He took it upon himself to make all the arrangements for Ernst's treatment and simply swamped our quarters with the best medical experts Moscow could offer – to Ernst's annoyance, having to undergo incessant examinations. He frequently visited him and was charming in his simplicity and warmth. It seemed a good sign for the policy of the forthcoming congress – Bukharin was now head of the Comintern – and Ernst felt reassured.

Our sanatorium with 600 patients and a huge staff of 400 doctors, nurses, workers, and cooks, was a self-contained institution which offered good grounds for observing social as well as personal relations. I came to the conclusion very soon that there was a very small margin indeed between deliberate social wrecking and smug, unshakeable indifference.

The place surpassed all our expectations. Medical care and food were far above the 'bourgeois' Swiss level. But there was some constant snag to irritate. The most vulnerable and annoying aspect was the food. Poultry and meat were too tough for consumption and thrown away in large quantities; soup and vegetables, stewed fruit were hardly touched. I spoke to our house-doctor. He complained about defects of supply and other matters beyond his control.

'But what about our chicken soup? You send up enormous plates of it and there is an unpardonable excess of water which makes it utterly tasteless. You cannot expect that much of a poor chicken. Everybody complains. Couldn't you give us small portions of some more nourishing substance instead? The same goes for your stewed fruit which is dissolved in too much water. Surely this does not depend on supplies.'

'It cannot be done', he said firmly. 'We are ordered to supply definite *quantities*. If we don't comply with regulations there might be complaints and we shall come under heavy fire.'

'But what about the other reasonable complaints. You are responsible for our health. You are a doctor.'

'We are helpless, we cannot change the regulations. Perhaps later on, in due time. Oh, but you can have anything you like. I shall immediately send you the chef to work out your menus.'

On Bukharin's personal orders we were to enjoy preferential treatment, food and all – which Ernst resolutely declined.

'The food is plentiful, but my husband has the same objections. He does not wish to break his teeth on it.'

There were other deficiencies, which were simple to correct, with workers, technicians and tools on the spot. To spare the patients the long walk to the house, a public convenience was thoughtfully erected on the beach, where we went daily to sunbathe. The seat was broken which made the use of it very difficult for the many crippled patients.

'It has been in this condition for at least two years', I was told by the old-timers. There were already quite a few accidents. I spoke to the doctor. He was very embarrassed – Russians don't talk about such matters. He made his notes but nothing happened. I was stern. He asked me to wait. The head doctor was due in a day or so, he had greater powers to order repairs. The new arrival was a highly intelligent cultivated man and a Bolshevik of old vintage. He often visited us and I soon mentioned my grievance. Nothing happened. I did it again. And again. He lost his temper: 'You West Europeans are terribly spoilt and make a fuss about nothing.'

'And I am determined to discover the hidden mechanism which hinders you from repairing that which any housewife would have done within days. I am prepared to carry the case to the highest authorities.'

It was late Saturday afternoon. There was no sunbathing on Sundays, but an excited girl patient came running to tell me that the great deed had been accomplished.

In general, things did not look as cheerful as on my last visit in 1925. There were many signs of overt discontent. The food situation was disquieting. The Government's promises of a good harvest particularly irritated the farmers who saw their crops vanishing before their eyes, evoking general cynicism. A change of mood could even be gauged from the behaviour of ordinary citizens. The word 'comrade' which was earlier used as a coveted distinction was now an expression of contempt: 'Of course it is good enough for *comrades*', and so on.

Hand-kissing and 'good manners' in the old style, reappeared. Nothing was left of the former adjustment to the language and ways of the 'proletarians'. On the contrary, the better situated comrades tried to live up to bourgeois standards.

Among the patients was a woman of the higher Party ranks. She complained that her child, a boy of 11, a pioneer of course, insisted on reading in the public library: 'I buy him any books he wants to keep him away. Think of the danger of mixing with ordinary children of low hygienic standards. But the boy does not appreciate the argument and cries and storms.' I told her I was sending my boy of twelve to a pioneer camp and I insisted on his travelling by himself. The term 'pioneer' should not be just another word. She was shocked but the other girls applauded.

The girls, so intelligent, so refreshing, ambitious, hardworking in spite of illness. Girl engineers, laboratory assistants, agronomists, mathematicians. And they were pathetically feminine in their irrepressible striving for beauty, so charmingly vain, even if they had to rely on spare accessories and on powder not much better than white flour. They were the product of the new order and compared so well with the women of my generation.

14.

The Wittorf Affair

The Sixth World Congress of the Comintern was taking place. Ernst used to say he was destined to attend the even-numbered congresses. Now he was in Russia, but not in Moscow to play his part. I was busily translating the Russian papers for him. So far the proceedings indicated no great changes. Even if only in mild terms, the Left's mistakes were criticised. The Congress spoke of 'a certain inclination to ignore United Front tactics, to misapprehend the immense importance of trade union activities and indulgence in the policy of revolutionary phraseology.' This was an acknowledgement that the fundamental errors for which the former leadership was declared 'ultra-left' had not been rectified. It was for the Left then to make amendments, although the fire was concentrated on the Right as the 'greater evil'.

There were matters which could not be easily gauged from the reports. If the formal resolutions left some room for fighting ultra-left policy, the leadership of the former Centre Group was accused of indulgence towards the Right, and they emerged from the Congress with the new suggestive title of 'Conciliators'.

Yet their struggle for unification of all loyal Communist forces was in perfect agreement with the decisions of the Executive and the Party. The re-admission to Party work of Thalheimer and Brandler was, moreover, a foregone conclusion. Ernst wrote to the

Politbureau in March 1928:

> Dear Comrades,
>
> I expect that Brandler and Thalheimer will certainly be considered for nomination in the forthcoming parliamentary elections.
>
> I wish to leave no doubts about the suitability of their candidacy.
>
> After the Executive agreed to allow them to carry out Party work there are no serious objections to them. The question of whether their work is correct at the present time has to be answered in the affirmative. Developments since Essen prove that to exclude comrades from Party work for their former serious dissensions with the Party, once these have passed, is harmful, and their co-option profitable. It would be shortsighted to shrink from difficulties for fear of the noise of the ultra-left.
>
> After the Central Committee rightly requested in its circular letter that the Party should stand up to the attacks of the Maslow people and the SPD against comrades Brandler and Thalheimer we must now draw the appropriate practical conclusions from that appeal. To what extent is our decision on Thalheimer's work in Germany actually being carried out ?
>
> With comradely greetings
>
> Ernst Meyer

By declaring the Right the greater evil and the Centre Group as suspicious intermediaries the Comintern gave full rein to the former ultra-left section of the Politbureau. Ernst's section was treated accordingly and a very disillusioned and embittered faction left the Congress. Their faith in the Russian leadership, shaken enough by its former errors, had gone. In retrospect, it dawned on them how futile it was to rely on arbitrary 'Open Letters' and on corrections from outside.

No sooner was the Congress over than it came to light that Wittorf, the political secretary of the Hamburg section, a brother-in-law and friend of Thaelmann, had embezzled 3000 marks from Party funds. The fact was known to Thaelmann but he conspired with two members of his devoted Hamburg clique to cover up the theft. It was not quite clear whether Thaelmann was motivated by fear or family loyalty. For Wittorf's appointment had been affected by Thaelmann's personal interference and against strong opposition.

The Conciliators grasped at this godsend. Despairing of the possibility of a square political struggle they resorted to a detour and staged a kind of a palace revolution. At an emergency session of the Central Committee they revealed the embezzlement and Thaelmann's role in the affair.

Thaelmann immediately put in his resignation, he confessed, he whined, he wept. The Central Committee was convinced that it was the end of Thaelmann and, to a man, deserted their leader. Only the smart Neumann was quick to grasp what Thaelmann's fall would mean to Stalin's prestige and decided to bide his time by abstaining from voting. It was chiefly on his advice that Thaelmann appealed to the Comintern. The matter then rested with the Almighty.

The assailants lost no time. The next day, 27 September, the world learned of the sordid affair from the Communist morning papers. We heard the news from a German comrade, Schumann, who brought us the *Rote Fahne*. He was another Comintern victim, kept on ice in Moscow like the more prominent Brandler and Thalheimer. Odd, inhibited, frustrated in his personal life, he lived only for the Party. Very unhappy in his exile, he was now convinced that he, along with his fellow sufferers, would soon be allowed to return home. He was planning, dreaming. There was a pathetic quietude in his manner, like the calm of a child recovering from a grave illness.

Ernst felt very uneasy from the start about the handling of the Wittorf case. He wrote to Karl Becker:

Crimea, 30 October 1928

Because of insufficient information I can only make the following remarks with reservations.

Though in no way indulgent towards T's behaviour, his errors must take second place to those of the Central Committee. I find it incomprehensible that they could think of publication, and especially at such a time, without the counsel of the Executive.

If they rightly intended to reduce Thaelmann's exceptional position to that of Ewert's they achieved exactly the opposite. Besides, consolidation, which requires a very tight unity with the former Left, is a political aim and a necessity for the Party as such and not alone for the 'Conciliators'. This goal does not depend on T's good will but must be struggled for by our own correct policy.

After 1923 I considered the block with the former Left as more important than the collaboration with Brandler and his associates. This was also expressed in my declaration of December 1926. I have no intention of departing from it, above all at a time when the 'production-controllers' (the Brandlerists) commit so many mistakes. In a choice between Brandler and Thaelmann I would have no hesitation. I consider the Brandler group obsolete and sectarian. The articles of the best of them (T) are the clearest evidence of it.

All this does not exclude, but explicitly includes, resistance to the new organisational measures, the political zigzag and the general passivity which marks the new course. I would define my position – always with reservation (lacking exact data):

1) formal acknowledgement of the erroneous decision of the Central Committee of September.

2) Precise demarcation from the Hansen Group. [A Right group. – RLM]

3) Intensified political activity (not only criticism, but suggestions and collaboration).

4) Fight for unification which includes a struggle against victimisation.

But neither Ernst, nor many other comrades, doubted that Thaelmann was finished. German workers are perhaps more exact than others in money matters and would not tolerate a leader in any way connected with embezzlement. The fall of Stalin's explicit nominee would also weaken his position in the eyes of the German workers and make criticism an easier task. And after the series of recent misjudgements there was reasonable hope that the Comintern would learn its lesson and leave it to the German Communists to produce and train their own 'historic leaders'.

Ernst was burning with impatience to return to Germany, where he thought he was needed more than ever – unhealed wound or not.

Perhaps it was my concern about my husband's health which made me more sceptical about the situation's urgency. But my doubts were sustained by very suggestive conversations with Russian comrades. So far the Russian papers had kept mum but Party members must have been informed and given some hints. They all virtually cursed the German 'pettiness': 'To make such a row about such a trifling sum of money.' It was quite a startling approach to the problem and it suddenly struck me that under no circumstances would Thaelmann be dropped. Stalin was too closely associated with him, it would shatter his own position and he is too powerful to let it happen. I submitted my argument to Ernst. He dismissed it categorically: 'Stalin is not alone. The question will be decided by the Politbureau. Who will *dare* to raise his hand in Thaelmann's favour? They cannot keep a man at the top of Germany's revolutionary movement who proved, to say the least, weak and unstable. Besides, he committed a gross breach of Party discipline by treating a Party affair in an arbitrary personal way. They don't tolerate such behaviour.'

It seemed conclusive but I was not convinced: 'I don't know *how* it will be done. Stalin is too involved; by some tricks and twists, he will make it.'

Ernst thought for quite a while and then said there was no need for headrolling at all. Stalin only had to treat the case from a political not a personal angle. How could such a situation arise? There were two great weaknesses in the leadership. One was Thaelmann's complete isolation. He had not one single person in the entire Central Committee to trust enough to discuss the calamity with, not even among his own close circle. The other was to regard and treat Hamburg as his private territory. Wittorf was appointed as a sort of viceroy and no other member of the Central Committee was allowed to penetrate that stronghold. Such a state easily breeds corruption and abuse of power. Had other leaders been able to work in Hamburg the embezzlement would hardly have taken place at all or at least could have been dealt with in a less disgraceful way. Ernst had always thought such a state untenable.

On the other side, Ernst continued, there were enough mistakes in handling the case by the Central Committee, albeit by his own group. Singling out the weak points all round, Stalin would do a service to the Party without damaging his own prestige or even, unreasonably, that of Thaelmann. Even if Stalin was not prepared to correct the decisions of the Sixth Congress as a whole, these mistakes could easily be exposed and criticised. Fatherly advice to go home and live henceforth in peace might even enhance Stalin's position.

But the verdict of the Comintern was as prompt as it was staggering, exceeding the most pessimistic expectations. No heed at all was paid to the facts. The affair was denounced as a vicious plot of irresponsible intellectuals, who, blinded by their lust for power, had not stopped at betraying the interests of the Party. Unfortunately, they had succeeded for a while in 'leading astray' the Central Committee which passed an incorrect resolution. But it quickly rectified its mistakes, and once more to a man: 25 of its members recanted on the 5th of October, as soon as they heard of the Comintern's decision; others, like Ulbricht, fell over themselves to prove that they had repented even earlier. Thaelmann was cleared and reinstated in his former position. And he was not in the least embarrassed about keeping it.

The verdict was a crude affront not only to decency but to reason itself and Stalin knew then that he could treat the German leaders like vassals in a conquered land. It was his first move, not in the interest of Soviet Russia – as his apologists contended – but for securing a mute servile Comintern.

And the 'German proletariat'? On my return to Berlin I asked a young Communist worker what his factory thought of it? They had been very depressed: what if the Central Committee decides today on a revolution and changes its mind tomorrow and calls it off? They were teased and mocked by the Social Democrats and felt embarrassed. They were satisfied though that Thaelmann was an honourable chap and rather pitied him. Thaelmann was a fellow worker and once the workers had accepted him as their leader there was class solidarity in their attitude towards him.

On hearing the verdict, Ernst was beside himself: 'I am leaving. I cannot stay here for another day. I won't accept hospitality from this government.'

He was still bed-ridden and could not move. I promised to make all the necessary preparations; as soon as he could travel we would leave. But where could we go from there? I shared his impulsive revulsion, but who were his hosts? Not Stalin, but the Russian people. It was also in their service that he had spent his health. The problem was wrongly posed and in my heart of hearts I hoped to persuade him to stay on.

15.

Return to Ultra-Left Policy, 1928

We spent some further weeks in the Crimea because the doctors categorically forbade Ernst to leave. But they favoured his removal to a more comfortable convalescent home. The place was populated by the cream of Soviet bureaucracy, mostly simple, devoted people with a blind faith in the Party. Many of them had favourites among the leaders now under fire. There was a blond man who had tried hard to model himself after Jaglom, with whom he was connected through the Civil War: 'Jaglom is now too good to mix with the rank and file! Jaglom has turned into an ambitious bureaucrat! . . . It is true Jaglom was often absent from the Party cell, but I never thought of it before. I was convinced that there was a good reason for it, but now . . .'

We became great friends, chiefly because of my friendship with his idol, and he often came to me to share his bitter disappointment. I tried to comfort him, but who was I to dispel the allegations of the Party?

The fear which I saw dwindling in 1922 and which seemed to have disappeared altogether in 1925 was unmistakably re-appearing, threatening human relations and above all, as I discovered in the sanatorium, the progress of the country. It was very disquieting, but my Russian friends laughed at me. Of course, they had difficulties, it was foolish to expect a straight road, but they were doing very well.

The November celebrations seemed to sustain the optimism. We went to the pioneer camp to lend the great event special significance. The pioneers prepared an elaborate show with songs and recitals. And dances! In a group of Russian children there will invariably be one or two to suggest a future Nijinsky or Pavlova. Who ever saw such celebrations? Even Ernst forgot his worries for a while. A Russian comrade said: 'Are you surprised? The spirit of a free and happy people is mirrored in the festivities.' He must be right, I thought. It is I, we, who fail to see the forest for the trees. Stalin is not everything.

Our stay in Russia coincided with the decisive changes of its post-revolutionary period – the end of the NEP and introduction of the Five Year Plan. We were also able to watch from close quarters Stalin's methods of crushing resistance and introducing a state in which the best Bolshevik leaders stopped asking where policy would lead but only what Stalin commanded. 'You cannot fight Stalin, he is too powerful' was heard more and more.

When we returned to Moscow, our quarters became a centre of the Russian opposition to the first Five Year Plan. They compared the scene with a stock exchange: heads of Russia's economy, science, Party, were trying to outbid each other by quoting higher and even higher targets. The campaign against Bukharin was strong enough indication that moderation or doubt would be stamped as 'opportunism' and lack of revolutionary spirit. The opposition was quite convinced that no one took the Five Year Plan seriously in its current form and that it was only a game to serve Stalin's dark purposes. They felt very strong and confident of their ultimate victory.

As was customary Ernst informed Stalin of his arrival in Moscow, putting himself at his disposal. It could be expected that Stalin would wish to see him, if not to hear his opinion, at least to try to win a loyal collaborator for himself in Germany. After all, Ernst was a member of the Politbureau and of the Executive itself. And he was absolutely 'innocent' of the Wittorf dealings. It is another measure of Stalin's contempt for persuasion and comradely collaboration as well as for traditional procedures that he did not seize such an opportunity.

The German Left, singled out to show its revolutionary superiority, resorted once more to bragging – so characteristic of Ruth Fischer's time. And the Bolshevik leaders, who knew by experience and theory the danger of fostering false illusions, encouraged them. In one characteristic episode, the Party described a strike against a lockout – a typical assault on workers whatever the reason may be as 'a revolutionary *offensive* against capitalists'. It happened while we were still in Moscow and Ernst protested. A long conversation with Gussev, a fellow member of the Executive, followed. Gussev had been a personal friend of Lenin, a distinguished revolutionary with a good command of revolutionary theory, who was soon to become head of the theoretical section of the Comintern. He had great sympathy for Ernst but was very annoyed. Their heated argument was leading nowhere. Pressed to the wall, Gussev, who played a prominent part in military affairs as well, resorted to a vague military term: 'Let us agree on calling it a concurrent encounter.'

'Not acquainted with military terminology, I wouldn't know its meaning', was Ernst's reply. 'Let us not play with words, but call things by their proper names and not make a laughing stock of our leadership . . .'

Ernst returned exhausted from the battle. But at the same time he was amused at the ingenuity of finding vague definitions, so reminiscent of Ruth Fischer's tricks. He entered the room laughing the way one does in anticipation of sharing a good joke. I knew this bitter laughter so well.

There was a method in such deliberate confusion. It was part of the theory of an acute revolutionary situation which, in the absence of facts, had to be sustained by spectacular declarations. Gussev apparently found it easier to accept nonsensical overtures by German leaders than to get involved in a fight against Stalin.

The sudden recourse to a full scale ultra-left policy did not have a political objective, but was a means of shaking off all 'undesirable elements'. There was not a shred of justification for re-establishing a policy, the abolition of which had shaken the KPD to the core only three years before. With all its defects and zigzagging the Party was making considerable progress, gaining in influence and authority. There was room neither for disappointment nor for immediate spectacular victories. It was not a contest for power but for influence over the social democratic workers, as its preparatory stage, 'winning over the majority of the organised workers'. The three essential points were: United Front tactics, trade union work and freedom of criticism or self-criticism as laid down the previous year at the Essen Party Conference.

These were the main bones of contention between the two groups. But it would have been impossible to discredit and oust the 'Conciliators' and other 'Rights' without claiming new historic changes, demanding new tactics. Thus a 'Third Period', using the bogey of an imminent war danger, turning the Social Democrats into 'Social Fascists', the trade unions into unassailable fortresses and so on, had to be invented to sustain the new tactics.

The artificiality of the new concepts is best shown by the resolutions of the Party congress of May 1929:

The changed international situation, the intensification of the class-struggle in Germany, the perspective of an imperialist war, the counter-revolutionary development of the SPD and chiefly the revolutionary upsurge of the workers' movement, makes it imperative that our Party adjust its tactics to the newly created conditions for struggle . . .

The essence of the tactical changes is a ruthless, bold attack against reformism, a transition from the agitational unmasking of the reformist traitors, from the stage of mere rallying and preparing the workers for the revolutionary struggle to the independent leadership of proletarian mass-actions against German imperialism.

This tactical orientation consists of applying new forms of revolutionary mass mobilisation, new forms of proletarian

United Front from below, new forms of fighting the bourgeoisie and reformism . . .

In conjunction with intensified oppositional work within the trade unions the Party will increasingly orientate itself towards new strata of the proletariat, the millions of unorganised workers.

Far from isolating the Party from the masses (as is being argued by the liquidationist-opportunistic Conciliators) these tactics fulfill the Leninist condition for the struggle for power – the winning of the majority of the proletariat in the key centres.

This policy does not signify a curtailment of the Bolshevist United Front policy, but rather the shifting of its weight to below, into the factories, the extension of the proletarian United Front far beyond the Social Democrats and trade union members to the majority of the proletariat as a whole.

The Party which must, with increased vigour take over the decisive struggle for winning over the majority of the working class and must pursue to the end the new general line of its tactics with all its means and against all its enemies.

In view of the dangers of war, fascism, and illegality the Party will strengthen its ties with the . . . exploited masses. The tactical line of the Party is clearly directed towards the revolutionary perspective of the impending struggle.

It was certainly true that the SPD's restraint of its members – *the organised* – was the greatest obstacle to the revolution. But it was at the same time an unwitting admission by the Party that it was they, rather than the unorganised workers, who counted. I was taught on many occasions to distinguish between the revolutionary value of organised and unorganised workers. Once I was carried away by the sight of a large demonstration.

'Too many housewives, women, youngsters', Ernst coolly remarked.

'What is wrong with women and youngsters', I asked, slightly piqued.

'Nothing. But for the revolution we need factory workers, organised in a party or at least in trade unions.'

'Even in a Social Democratic party?' I was also inclined to favour 'the revolutionary unorganised'.

'Even there.' He argued this was proof that they realised things ought to be changed and were prepared to do something about it. They read papers, attended meetings, paid their weekly contributions. They were no longer an amorphous faceless mass. They had taken the first step and it was our task to persuade them to go further. The more sincere part of the unorganised felt rather guilty for sitting on the fence and letting others do the job. Now they were being flattered and told that they were superior to the rotten Social Democratic followers. They gloried in their new role, and felt superb if they occasionally attended our demonstrations or meetings. But we could not rely on them for any action. We would either bring to our side those erring organised workers, caught in the net of a strong flourishing organisation, or there would be no revolution. These were the best we had, with no other sources to draw from.

Vehemently fighting the Conciliators for upholding this truism, even Thaelmann suddenly advised the Party to go a step further and more resolutely and energetically draw in the *qualified* workers who constituted the strongest element of the organised (a section always regarded as least accessible to revolutionary propaganda). He even drew the proper conclusion such a victory might afford the Party: 'The more we succeed in achieving it the better we shall win over the unorganised.' But such insights were short-lived and quickly forgotten.

It is true that a crisis was maturing in Germany. In 1928 there was an alarming growth of unemployment and unmistakable restlessness on all levels. But this only called for more boldness in the application of proven old tactics. And the Sixth Congress found it necessary to upbraid the Party for deficiencies on exactly this point.

The turn to the Left was so sudden that even the clever Walter Ulbricht was unable to keep pace. A loyal follower of the Centre Group he testified, as late as November 1928, that he knew of no single case where the 'Conciliators' supported the Right. He soon recovered his balance though and hastily joined in hunting them. On 1 December 1928 he wrote to Ernst from Moscow:

> You informed me that because of the bad weather conditions and the overstrain of the last session of the Polit-Secretariat you intended to leave for Berlin on 3 December. I think that it is necessary for you to stay on until the next session of the Polit-Secretariat. My reasons are the following:
>
> 1) After you and Comrade Humbert-Droz made an attempt to develop a platform against the line of the Comintern and the Central Committee at the last session of the Polit-Secretariat, it is absolutely necessary for you to hear the ideas of the members of the Secretariat and to take cognizance of any answer.
>
> 2) I believe that if your physical condition permitted you to speak for $1\frac{1}{4}$ hours you are certainly strong enough to listen to the answer.
>
> Should you nevertheless leave on Monday, such untimely departure could only be regarded as an attempt to avoid clarifying your attitude to the resolution of the Polit-Secretariat about the policy of the German Communist Party.
>
> With comradely greetings
The German Representation of the ECCI
Walter Ulbricht

Ernst answered:

Moscow, 3 December 1928

> Without questioning the high political qualities of Comrade Ulbricht, who so perceptively discovered that my defence of the theses of the Sixth Congress against the falsifications of the Central Committee majority was a platform against the Comintern, I do not have enough confidence in Ulbricht's

medical opinion. I cannot therefore postpone my necessary
and already overdue departure any longer.
Besides, even today I was unable to find out when the continuation
of the session would definitely take place.

With comradely greetings
Ernst Meyer

Ernst's answer to Ulbricht is not merely an expression of
his contempt. The new line was introduced so cautiously and the
confusion so great that for a while Ernst's group could accuse the
leadership of violating the resolutions of the last congress. The less
initiated leaders found it very difficult to grasp exactly what was
demanded of them. It did not last, however. They soon learned to repeat Stalin's orders with automatic precision, and find theoretical
foundations for his crooked 'line'.

16.

The Battle of Mayday, 1929

We arrived back in Berlin in December, 1928, Ernst still with an unhealed wound. I tried in vain to shield him from too many visitors and upsets; neither could I keep him from Central Committee sessions or even conferences outside Berlin. In view of his bad health his group held its meetings in our home and I was always present as 'a silent partner'. The house was swarming with alarmed and bewildered people, trying to find an explanation for the new policies. 'No reason, no reason at all', was not a comforting answer. The situation was far worse than it was in Ruth Fischer's time. Never before was the leadership given such unqualified support by the Comintern. Under Zinoviev it had been in no mood to dispose of Ernst's group. But now the Comintern was in Stalin's hands, and his treatment of the Wittorf affair made it clear that any opposition would face expulsion.

Could the Centre Group stand the test? Some remarks, vague asides and silences suggested a disturbing answer. Karl Becker, when hard pressed, passionately exclaimed: 'Never shall I allow myself to be cut off from revolutionary Russia.' Some others, Eberlein among them, looked embarrassed. When similar hints piled up I drew my conclusions and bluntly declared to Ernst: 'I fully agree with everything you say. I shall follow you to the end. But you must measure your steps in accordance with your own strength.

They will desert you. As a group you will fail. It is a *political* error to rely on its support, and if it comes to a vote in my Party cell I shall cynically vote against you. I am not prepared to make all the sacrifices in vain.'

My suspicions were confirmed when, one day, Humbert-Droz arrived from Moscow to see if Bukharin could rely on the support of the group. Volk looked embarrassed: 'Rely on us ? We are powerless, insignificant, nothing'. This declaration of powerlessness carried the unmistakable stamp of capitulation, and the silence of the rest of the group was a bad omen, suggesting they knew in advance that they would surrender. Visitors tried to persuade Ernst to abstain from criticism: 'What if you are expelled ?' 'Isn't it your duty to stick to the banner at all cost ?' 'You must preserve yourself for the future – you just have to bide your time.'

There could be no question of coming to terms with the perilous new Party line. But it was Ernst's conviction that he must try to fight from within, that an opposition has to go to the limit to avoid expulsion on 'legalistic' disciplinary ground. The group, therefore, professed that: 'In spite of the victimisation of our adherents, in spite of the false political course and errors, vacillations in the execution of the resolution of the Sixth Congress, we shall do everything in our power to re-establish the unity of the Party.'

Unfortunately, at this crucial moment, Brandler decided to return to Germany in open defiance of the Comintern. His breach of discipline was a great blow to the opposition camp. After some six years of submission, even ignoring an invitation to appear before a special Commission to argue his case, Brandler now aggravated his own position and, moreover, forced Ernst's group to over-emphasise its dissociation from him, with the inevitable result of making too many concessions to the Comintern. They even endorsed the Comintern's view that Brandler was 'the main danger'.

The 'fight for unity' in Ernst's declaration was essentially a struggle against Brandler's expulsion from the Party. The group neither condoned Brandler's hasty action, nor refrained from opposing his political ideas. But they insisted on 'a thorough preliminary political debate' and adequate warnings against factional activities. Only then would they agree to enforce disciplinary measures:

Berlin, 19 December 1928

To the Politbureau

Dear Comrades,

The editions of the *Rote Fahne* on the 16th, 18th and 19th of December, devoted to the last Control Committee session, prove that the Politbureau is persevering in its attempts to mislead the Party on internal matters. The suppression of Ewert's and my declaration serves only the Right. They are kept ignorant of the fact that the 'Conciliators' oppose their political ideas and, should they refuse to relinquish their factional activities, would, after an adequate preliminary political debate, also favour their expulsion. A Central Committee that does not wish to make itself guilty of favouritism towards the Right should have used precisely *this* fact against them, and also informed the Party, instead of giving the false impression that the 'Conciliators' are against disciplinary measures.

The decision of the Central Control Committee, printed in Sunday's *Rote Fahne*, by the way, confirms the views which Ewert and I have proposed primarily to the Central|Committee session as the most appropriate method of liquidating the Right faction. Comrade Ewert and I have therefore dispatched to the ECCI the following telegram:

Comintern Moscow,

Urgent request to reconsider Central Committee resolution concerning Walcher; to amend conditions and extend time limit Stop. Consider application of Central Committee's decisions would endanger and eventually lead to a loss of important trade union positions in Stuttgart, Hanau, Solingen and of hundreds of functionaries Stop. Ewert arrives Thursday. Ernst Meyer.

With comradely greetings
Ernst Meyer

The fight against the Conciliators was steadily increasing in provocation, and Ernst protested and fought for his rights. He did not expect fair treatment, but he used every vestige of legality to make his own expulsion as difficult as possible. His faith in the Comintern had gone, but he felt that a small opposition group should remain for the workers to turn to when the Party had played itself out again.

A war of attrition began with infuriating petty tricks. On his return to Berlin he was refused a meeting with the Politbureau:

Charlottenburgh, 12 December 1928

To the Politbureau
    Dear Comrades,
Despite my repeated requests to have an opportunity for a confidential conversation with the Politbureau this has, so far, been rejected. The Politbureau then refuses either to inform me, *who was absent more than a year*, or take cognizance of my political views. This is also a *political* issue as much as the fact that the Politbureau failed to send me *any information* since last June — for 6 months — in spite of my repeated requests.
I therefore categorically demand an immediate meeting today with the Politbureau (before the start of the Central Committee plenary), and am waiting for a telephone call (Steinplatz 14494) to this effect.

With comradely greetings
Ernst Meyer

Nearly every day Ernst wrote protests and threats to the Politbureau:

Berlin, 19 December 1928

    Dear Comrades,

The composition of speeches designed for Party meetings in commemoration of the 10th KPD anniversary, written by Comrade Gelber and sanctioned by C. Lenz, is a *model of factional falsification of history*. Almost every page is filled with the grossest errors, distortions and twists to suit the

Ultra-Left policies *and* its faction. The 'Left', Ruth Fischer
faction is exempted from all criticism while *all* other Party
trends and the Party itself are discredited.

This composition, which by far surpasses Maslow's falsification of
Party history, is another demonstration of the Central Com-
mittee's failure to put up the slightest resistance against
Ultra-Left views.

I protest most emphatically against this shameful document, demand its immediate withdrawal and, should it be rejected,
forward at once my protest to the propaganda section of
the ECCI.

With comradely greetings
Ernst Meyer

No immediate expulsion was threatened and the group
stood firm, made resolutions of its own, opposed the 'Central Committee majority', criticised. The group at this time contained two of
the five members of the Politbureau as well as several members of
the Central Committee, all men whose political and theoretical
weight far exceeded that of the ruling body. Nevertheless, Ernst
was nearly convinced of his inevitable expulsion, when an unexpected event occurred to change the picture. The 1st of May was approaching and the socialist chief of police, Zoergiebel, issued an order prohibiting all street demonstrations. Only closed meetings
were permitted for the traditional yearly celebrations. The workers
were deeply humiliated, but Zoergiebel was unperturbed, counting
on the deep split which the new Communist tactics produced
among the workers and on the Party's self-induced isolation.

The Communists called for a demonstration and even
Ernst expected strong support against the outrage. In the middle of
April he wrote to the Politbureau, advising that those Communists
still belonging to the trade unions be encouraged to attend the pre-
dominantly Social-Democratic union meetings. It would be the
best place to remind the workers of their class solidarity, and
appeal to them, at the end of the meeting, to join in the
demonstration. To achieve immediate contact with the workers he

suggested that the timing of the demonstrations coincide with the end of the meetings.

It was not at all a simple matter. Thaelmann said it would be very wrong to *split* our forces by sending away our trade union members. As for the timing — well, he implied, the others could come if they wanted to. What could one expect of 'social fascists' ?

The demonstration was a catastrophic failure. Even the Party members did not turn up in force. The police were easily able to beat up the few demonstrators, even singling out the poorly dressed and less 'respectable' for special treatment. They spared our large column, coming from the better part of Berlin, and looking more solvent.

It could hardly be called a demonstration by any standards, with only individuals running in all directions, pursued by raving police. There was not a single leader to give direction, to address the crowd, or make one moment's stand. It was a cruel awakening for the Party leadership and their attempt to find scapegoats fell flat. Eyewitnesses spoke of a very bewildered Central Committee in complete disarray.

In the late afternoon shots were heard in the workers' district. No one knew what was happening. The tension caused by the demonstration was still in the air, and wild rumours circulated — an uprising? Our telephone rang incessantly. Ernst tried to communicate with the Central Committee, but could not get an articulate answer.

Next morning the Communist papers screamed: 'Barricades in Berlin!' 'The proletariat against Zoergiebel's police!' In fact, there were 'barricades in Berlin', when people in panic tried to stop the penetration of police into their localities. But the improvised barricades were neither manned nor armed, and were not a product of deliberate revolutionary action. In the end, twenty-nine people were killed, but not one policeman hurt.

The Party tried to present the carnage as an act of heroic resistance to the police, a repetition of the Hamburg Barricades of 1923: 'The Communist Party proudly identifies itself with the barricade fighters who put up active resistance to the brutal police of the social fascist Zoergiebel.' The Comintern came to their aid by flooding the Russian papers with accounts of the rising revolutionary spirit of the German proletariat. It was natural that the Communist Party should see justice done, but even the call for a 24-hour protest strike on the day of the victims' funeral found no response. Worse yet, many mourners, in whose defence the Party ostensibly acted, refused any association with it.

17.

Capitulation of the 'Conciliators'

The forthcoming Twelfth Party Congress was postponed to give the leaders time to recover from the shock. In spite of the approval in the Russian press, they feared the Comintern might not forgive them such a defeat.

As for the opposition, Ernst reasoned that under the dismal circumstances the Comintern would not be inclined to cut off another influential section of the Party, and he tried, in endless debates, to convince his collaborators that there was no immediate danger of expulsion. He was due back in hospital but, anxious to stiffen their resistance, he decided not to leave the group before the end of the congress.

A Party congress was traditionally preceded by an exchange of opinion and discussions. Ernst immediately sent his contribution, wryly trying to avoid the leading body's tricks for curtailing freedom of expression:

Berlin, 11 April 1929

I have written the following article for the *Rote Fahne* and already
    sent it at the end of February to the Central Committee.
Since the Central Committee has only now permitted the publica-
    tion of Party discussions, my article does not deal with ques-
    tions which have, in the meantime, moved to the centre of
    the debates.

Party members who, in view of the massive assaults of the Central
Committee majority, might find my language tame, should
take into consideration that the Central Committee majority, accusing me dozens of times of 'political cowardice',
have, in advance made the publication of *my* article con-
ditional on my 'tone'. I was therefore forced to avoid the
opposite sharpness.

Ernst Meyer

The Left ruled supreme. In June 1929 Thaelmann entered
the hushed conference hall in the Stalin manner. Doors were opened wide and he appeared flanked and followed by a suite of his
faithful 'subordinates' – a king among his subjects. Everybody
looked very embarrassed, including Thaelmann himself, not yet
used to protocol.

Ernst, pale and shaky, also made his appearance. His
speech was hailed by the non-Communist press as the only one
worth listening to. He had not impressed the audience though,
mostly newcomers who knew nothing of him or his role in the
Party. One of them screamed: 'Where were you during the war and
the revolution?' And another: 'What have you in common with the
Party at all?'

He answered: 'I was wherever the Party thought fit to place
me – as I hope you too always fulfill your duty towards the revolution.' And: 'The short time allotted to me is not quite sufficient to
speak of my dissentions. It would take infinitely more to speak of
my bonds with the Party.'

It was his last public appearance.

The Centre Group was to present to the congress a platform of their own. But Ernst was becoming more conscious of the
group's instability and warned them against taking steps which
they might not be willing to defend to the last. They insisted on
working out a platform and became increasingly irritated by Ernst's
hesitation, regarding it as a personal insult. A number of people
were then assigned to deal with separate subjects like capitalist stab-

ilisation, war danger and so on. The finished article was a perfect abstract treatise, but concrete problems or the new Party line were hardly touched or criticised only by implication.

It was not contempt for theory which made me view the document with suspicion and scepticism. I saw before me the delegates, hand-picked men, chosen for their ignorance and fed on vulgar and meaningless Party publications. They were not qualified to judge complicated issues, and could hardly be expected to read the platform at all.

The 'platform' was doomed in advance. There was still time for correction, but it would have meant a frontal attack against the Almighty, and the group preferred a vague, non-committal method. When the platform appeared in the same issue with the official answer, misintepreted, pulled to pieces, it only gave the Central Committee another pretext for vilification and for creating greater animosity.

An article appeared in the Communist press, demanding unequivocal support for existing Party policy, and the group assembled for another session. I realised Ernst would advocate a position leading to expulsion. Noticing the stony faces of the group, I decided to leave the room.

At about 3 a.m. Ernst woke me up: 'They have just left, they all left me.' He spoke it like a death sentence, and for a while we both sat motionless, silent, stricken.

'What should I do now?', he asked pathetically.

Suddenly, the phone rang. It was Ewert. He was terribly sorry, it was a heated debate and a hasty step. He would like to come back for a minute. Ernst let him in. They had a very short conversation. Ewert said he was in complete agreement with Ernst. He apologized again, it must have been the strain. Ernst, for his part, made a few concessions: if hard pressed they might go so far as to abstain from factional activities for a *limited period*, but he insisted on making it quite clear that under no conditions would they revise their views or policy.

Ernst undertook to put it in writing, and Ewert left. Why

did he come ? They were out to capitulate — why did they make concessions instead of shaking Ernst off ? It made no sense to me.

Ernst tried to find the best formulation for his statement. At about 5 o'clock in the morning he jumped out of bed to put on paper what seemed to him a particularly happy expression. Terribly exhausted, he was afraid he might forget it.

Ewert turned up as promised, at 9 o'clock in the morning. He approved of Ernst's note, yes, it was excellent. Ernst cautioned: 'I shall be waiting by the telephone. Should any unforeseen situation arise, any complication, ring and I shall come immediately.'

In the early afternoon we were inundated with telephone calls: 'The capitulation of the Conciliators'. No word from Ewert or any of the friends. And none of them ever showed up again as long as Ernst was alive. Ewert had reappeared in the dead of night because without the faked agreement between them they would be obliged to exclude Ernst's name from their public declaration, which would make the capitulation far less effective.

Ernst's position was desperate. At that stage, he could not make any public declarations. It seemed more than quixotic to declare war on a ruthless enemy, as a *lonely individual* from a *hospital bed*, unable to follow through with any action. He merely informed the Central Committee of his departure to hospital – nothing more.

18.

The 'Red Trade Unions'

The hospital was close to Berlin, just outside Potsdam, but Party turmoil could not intrude there. This made it easier to take a broad view, in theory, of the new political situation. Brandler was gaining ground again. In a relatively short time he mustered some 10,000 supporters and issued a weekly paper; Ernst regarded his influence as dangerous. An opposition was necessary, but only if based on correct principles and tactics – 'a Leninist opposition'. Striving for mere numbers, for example, was short-sighted and futile. He would not therefore join Brandler.

Ernst admired Brandler's energy and never doubted his sincere bonds with the revolution, but thought his Right inclination very real. Brandler never renounced his October policy which had caused the ominous swing to the ultra-left.

For Ernst, there was an obvious, political choice, to stage that clarifying campaign for which he struggled throughout the years. It could not now be done through Party channels. Brandler no more admitted controversial opinion in his paper than did the Party itself – least of all from Ernst. Their old feud was not forgotten and Ernst's recent attacks were not designed for comradely discussions. Ernst therefore intended to create a forum of his own, even if a modest one to start with. As soon as he left hospital . . .

The Party was steadily moving towards full scale ultra-left policy. Some time at the end of May 1929, the *Rote Fahne* published the slogan: 'Beat the fascists wherever you find them.' Ernst sat up with a jolt, forgetting his wound: 'Fist fighting again! But it means putting ourselves outside the law. Whatever they do to us now there is no room for appeal.'

To one of the more sincere well-wishers who tried to persuade him, shortly before his death, to adapt himself to the 'line', he answered: 'I thought, let me forget all I had learned, make myself a blank and see what Molotov has to say about the term "social-fascism". But his article teaches: instead of busying ourselves with the definition of "social-fascism", comrades, let us just fight it – I flung the paper to the other corner of the room and that was that.'

One of the chief indications of ultra-left policy was once again the drive to form independent trade unions. This was nourished by the attitude of the trade unions themselves which, on many occasions, let down the workers and forced them into independent actions and 'illegal' strikes. Large numbers of workers were victimized and of necessity organized themselves into independent groups. At the time of the inauguration of Left rule in 1924 such groups existed in many industrial centres. Undoubtedly hostility to the unions was also stimulated by their counter-revolutionary attitude during the Reich's intervention in Saxony-Thuringia. Disappointment went far beyond the Communist ranks, and Ruth Fischer was quick to declare that 'the German workers lost their faith in the reformist trade unions for good', setting her course on independent revolutionary organisations.

Yet the fall of the Left at that time was chiefly a result of their trade union policy. Therefore, the revival of 'Red Trade Unions' was now introduced with great caution. It was ostensibly a means of building a collective centre for members expelled by the trade union bureaucracy – little more. Lozovsky, the head of the Red Trade Union International, RGI, explained:

In view of continuous impertinent divisive practices of reformist leaders and the growing antagonism between them and the

broad working masses, the adherents of the RGI in Germany must now consistently direct their course towards consciously and indefatigably organising a revolutionary trade union movement.
All activities must be subordinated to creating *independent organs of such a movement from top to bottom.*

These resolutions seemed to be offset by the explicit command to continue the work *within the trade unions*, for a complete departure from original Leninist tactics was impossible. Yet Losovsky unmistakably decreed the creation of independent trade unions and the Party obediently responded: 'The Central Committee welcomes the resolutions of the ECCI presidium to strengthen and extend the revolutionary trade unions.'

This was soon followed up with customary boasts: 'We are consistently heading towards building red trade unions all over Germany . . . In a few months we have mustered our first quarter of a million members and organised, at a stroke, factory groups in 3500 plants . . . The RGO (Revolutionary Trade Union Opposition) is increasingly . . . organising millions of workers, isolating the social democratic leaders and winning the majority of the working classes.'

The Party also supplied a 'theoretical' foundation for the new tactics: 'Through their ties with the capitalist system and the responsibility they assumed for its economy, the reformist and Christian trade unions are no longer capable or willing to conduct the necessary struggle for better wages and working conditions . . . This is why the RGO had to be created.'

Though consenting to work in the old trade unions ostensibly 'to gain positions and revolutionise the workers', this task was nullified by declaring it impossible to 'remove a single trade union official in a democratic manner. The trade union apparatus cannot be won over for defending the interests of its members. Who should then fight for the German workers ? . . . A new power is rising . . . the revolutionary RGO which is building, with the help of the Communist Party, a powerful revolutionary trade union movement on German soil . . .'

The rank and file genuinely hated the trade unions, especially after the leaders defined their membership not as erring brothers, but as 'fascist beasts'. And the Party encouraged this mood:

> It is clear that our argument with social-fascism as well as with the bourgeoisie, whose faithful servant it is, will not be settled at negotiation tables but on the battlefield of decisive struggle and at the revolutionary tribunals of the German Soviet Republic . . . The small functionary is an important, indeed the most important part of the social democratic apparatus, which became an essential part of the social-fascist state machine. He grumbles but just by grumbling he keeps the whole apparatus intact . . . Our heavy offensive against the big Zoergiebels can therefore only be successful if accompanied by a simultaneous assault on the bourgeois-infected small functionaries . . . We must clear the proletarian ranks of all rotten elements. He who still belongs to the SPD is rotten and must be sent packing despite his ever so radical talk.

The 'clearance work' went further: 'Drive the Social Fascists from their jobs in the factories and trade unions!' 'Chase them away from the factories, labour exchanges and professional schools.' It was only natural to conclude: 'Workers! Join the Red Unity Organisations! To remain in the reformist trade unions means sharing in the complicity of the reformist bureaucracy and betraying the workers' interests.'

The Communists left the trade unions as fast as they could. 'The first quarter of a million' consisted almost entirely of those faithful comrades. Despite talk of 'attacking the trade unions from within' the Party encouraged and provoked the desertion. In dealing with the elections of factory councils, the Party now demanded separate 'Red Lists'. One factory cell achieved great renown for disobeying the order and figuring on collective lists. But the Party was very vigilant in such matters of 'opportunist deviations', sitting in solemn judgement over the offenders and ordering their expulsion from the organisation. Their protests were of no avail.

The much-publicised independent unions turned out a failure. Thaelmann admitted 'self-critically' that there was much room for improvement and that 'the red unions, generally speaking, have not come up to expectations as a developing revolutionary fighting power . . . there is stagnation in the RGO. Workers who leave the trade unions don't join it.' He vehemently attacked the mischievous 'groups outside the Party who allege that the Red unions are only part of another Communist shop'. But unfortunately the same view was corroborated by the ECCI: 'The revolutionary trade union organisations have often no independent life and are turning into doubles of Party organisations with the same personnel mechanically repeating Party decisions.'

The Party used every means to keep the RGO going, coaxing, abuse, threats, shameless publicity and low membership fees, but the old trade unions stood firm. Thaelmann had learned from Stalin how to extricate himself from an ugly situation by blaming subordinates. 'Some people', he said, went too far in their 'uncovering' of social fascists: '. . . It was wrong, for instance, when members of reformist unions were sometimes regarded as homogeneous reactionary masses. It means stamping millions of social democratic workers as counter-revolutionaries and strike breakers. It was scandalous to identify them with the reformist bureaucracy. With such views one is naturally unable, given the weakness of the red unions and the RGO, to create victorious strikes.'

The Comintern had also suffered pangs of despair and was equally caught in its own mistakes. They knew the remedy and attempted quietly to switch over to the old tactics: '. . . Without systematic persistent and well organised daily work within the revolutionary trade unions as well as reformist and other reactionary trade unions it is impossible to win the majority of workers . . . The resolutions clearly explain that the building of a broad oppositional movement *within* those organisations is one of the conditions for rapid development of the independent revolutionary trade union movement, for the growth of the RGO and the red unions.'

This too could not be achieved without a thorough change of cadres and an honest dismissal of incorrect slogans: 'A broad oppositional movement within' is incompatible with the creation of external organisations and invalidates their usefulness. An opposition within was always considered a sufficient weapon for pressing reformist leaders to greater militancy.'

But this aspect was dangerously reminiscent of the slogan 'Forcing the bosses'. Since the Comintern had declared this slogan opportunistic, the workers might rightly conclude that there was then no more time to waste on the reactionary trade unions. The Comintern called such people 'left-sectarians' and declared: 'The Communist sections must relentlessly fight those "left-sectarians" within the parties and RGO who use the Comintern's fight against the opportunist slogan, "Force the bosses", for refusing to work within the reformist trade unions.'

At the same time, Thaelmann had to admit that without 'the bosses' nothing could be done: 'When the trade union leaders don't call a strike we are not able to do it on our own.'

One condition after another for building separate trade unions was quietly nullified. But no one dared condemn the bankrupt idea itself because this would mean a victory for the 'Conciliators and other Rights'.

19.

Death of Ernst Meyer, 1930

The hospital where the 'Reichs Insurance for Employees' accommodated its members turned out a remarkably satisfactory place. For several months Ernst had a room to himself; food and treatment were excellent. Bundles of books were dispatched to him weekly from the Prussian Diet. And soon he was allowed to go out for walks and even for occasional visits home.

For the time being our financial position was secure. Ernst received remuneration as a member of the Prussian Diet; only part of this was kept, since it was customary for Communists to surrender to the Party anything in excess of the established 'Party maximum'. In case he was expelled, Ernst was resolved to return his mandate to the Party, and this became a very controversial subject. Wouldn't it be more appropriate to keep the mandate – and money – to have a free hand for oppositional activities? Perhaps. But, Ernst argued, in the eyes of the workers this would look like scrambling for position and gain. I had to condition myself for a scraping existence and for the first time learned the art of saving. I knew that any work of mine, even translations, would be sabotaged by Party institutions. This was confirmed by Stoecker, who once exclaimed, after hearing some of my Russian experiences: 'But why don't you write about it? Our press needs such articles.' I played the innocent: 'Do you really think so? With such a warm recommenda-

tion of a member of the Central Committee the *Rote Fahne* is sure
to accept them in spite of Neumann.' The name had its intended effect. Stoecker stammered that the press was not really his department and of course Neumann was not likely to give publicity to the
wife of Ernst Meyer. I was merciless and argued about his duty to
protect a comrade against unjust victimisation. I knew it was in
vain, I was only driven by a desire to expose his servility and make
him aware of his sorry position in the Party.

Only after Ernst's death was I permitted paid Party work.

Unemployment was growing and, unlike Ruth Fischer's
period in a more stabilised Germany, the new Left line seemed to
work wonders. Thaelmann was given power in a rapidly deteriorat-
ing country and the Party was steadily growing in numbers. Yet it
remained the same Party with the same ideology and methods. Its
life consisted mainly of boasts, brawls and hunting infidels. Nor
had numerical growth prevented mental stagnation, cynicism and
corruption. The leaders thought nothing of making senseless demands which cost workers and employees their jobs and even endang-
ering lives by worthless assignments.

Another disturbing symptom was an indescribable reckless-
ness in the treatment of comrades. Once a visitor came to see Ernst
'just for sympathy'. He explained that he had been removed from
his journalist's job without any reason or explanation. Submitting
his complaint directly to Thaelmann, he was told: 'You were very
lucky to hold such a good job. You are not the only one unemployed
and should not fuss about it.' It was more than losing a job. This
man had broken all ties with his well-off family to become a Communist. Now he felt coldly pushed aside, with nowhere to go. For
his Communist friends a sacked colleague was a dead man.

The Party also continued hunting and abusing the Conciliators regardless of their capitulation. It goes without saying that
none of the Party leaders ever visited Ernst in hospital, or even
inquired after his health. And this included friends like Pieck who
had spent a life with him in the Party.

The doctors were pressing for another operation and we were preoccupied with the problem. According to the surgeon, it was to be another perfectly harmless affair, 'no worse than cutting a finger'; he grew very impatient with our indecision. Ernst was particularly reluctant to undergo another operation and he hesitated to the last. It was fixed for Monday morning and we were still discussing it on my Saturday visit. It seemed absurd to inflict pain and discomfort upon oneself without hope of improvement. But there was no use for further contemplation: 'I know, you have made your decision', I said at our parting. All day Sunday I had to fight an urge to see him. 'Cutting a finger' – this could be done under local anaesthetic. I meant to bring this up, but had somehow forgotten. It would have been useless anyway, since the surgeon was set on a decisive operation. I discovered later that the Russian surgeons, finding in the process that going further would endanger Ernst's life, had stopped an earlier operation. The German surgeon knew this but did not shrink from taking the risk. He told me afterwards that he considered it his duty to spare the patient the misery of a lingering illness.

His whole attitude was ambiguous and indefensible by accepted standards of medical ethics. This was the opinion of a number of non-Communist doctors, and the Russians found stronger expression for an operation they called 'death under the knife'.

On Monday I was informed that the operation was very successful. I saw Ernst next day according to schedule. He seemed more affected than after his former operations but I was not unduly worried. I was not even startled when the matron suggested that I should see the surgeon. 'It is rather customary', she insisted. After the usual exchanges the surgeon said: 'I very much hope we will pull him through.' Was there any doubt ? It must be a medical expression, and I stubbornly refused to comprehend. Next day I found Ernst in high fever, and in a semi-conscious state. Every conceivable complication had set in and he was visibly fading away. A mysterious wall was steadily growing between us. He was retiring into a world of his own with increasingly less room for me. Once he asked me to go away. 'Come tomorrow.' Sometimes he violently accused the staff of giving him the wrong drinks. 'It tastes strange. I don't trust them.' Once I found him singing the 'Internationale' as loudly as his wasting powers permitted. 'I do it often, it does not matter now', he reassured me, 'I can do whatever I like.'

I let myself be persuaded not to move to the hospital: 'He is unconscious most of the time.' 'You cannot stay in his room for long stretches.' 'He will notice your presence and it might frighten him.'

Towards the end, they kept me away from his bed: 'He will not recognise you.' I was numbed and had no will of my own. My knees trembled and I sat down on a chair. I was waiting – for what ? The silence was eerie, more so through the sounds of his rumbling breath. I heard them once from my dying father. A fly was buzzing – so unbearably alive. The flowers were alive too – he meant to enjoy them 'tomorrow'.

I was suddenly startled by a deep silence. They were doing something to his face. It was over. I was allowed to come nearer. He was calm and his face was strangely regaining its familiar shape.

Once more our flat was filled with people, Ernst's former friends appearing along with many others unknown to me. The family arrived, his old mother, brother and sister and his two sons. Telegrams, messages, flowers came from everywhere. Klara Zetkin sent her wreath to me, not wanting to mix with the Party leaders she despised.

The funeral was fixed for Thursday and the Party sent the programme of procedures for my approval. Until then Ernst was to lie in state in the Party headquarters. He was then to be buried beside Franz Mehring, whose friend and favourite disciple he was. This was Pieck's idea, his only spontaneous expression of emotion for an old comrade.

Eberlein was suspicious of the funeral plans: 'It only looks good on paper but they . . . cannot give him his due. Even the dead Ernst Meyer is a threat to them, I know them well. We must watch them carefully.'

It was worse than expected. Pieck was assigned to write the obituary and described Ernst essentially as a faithful pupil of Hilferding; all his thinking was influenced by his mentor. Hilferding, the economist, had influenced a generation of Party members, and even after the Revolution Lenin said that no serious Communist could afford to neglect his writings. But a world of controversy separated the Communists from Hilferding, who was a social-democrat, and by an ugly sleight-of-hand Pieck obliterated some fifteen years of Ernst's bitter fight against his former teacher. It was in fact a defamation entirely in the vein of Neumann and Muenzenberg, another accusation of 'siding' with enemies of Communism.

'But as a co-founder of the Spartakus League Ernst declared war on Hilferding in 1914', I told Pieck. 'Ernst was chosen to assist in working out the twenty-one points to keep the Hilferdings away from the Communist Party.' Pieck remained silent, knowing what the Party expected of him. I threatened: 'Comrade Pieck, this article must not appear or I will make the greatest scandal Berlin has ever known. I warn you, in my state, I am ready for anything.'

He was frightened and apologised. If it upsets me so much he promises to omit the passage.

A photo was to appear with the obituary, and I was asked to choose the one I liked best. It had already been set for printing when it was suddenly withdrawn. Apparently they could not show it since it was a good picture. A distorted picture of Ernst, copied from a holiday-snap, was more suitable for their purposes.

It was customary to appeal to the workers to honour their dead comrade. But this time the Party only indicated the route of the funeral procession in small print on an inside page. The confusion was compounded by a change in the time-table. The Party's excuse for this sabotage tactic was that street demonstrations were at that time forbidden, and it would be wrong to expose the workers to any danger of maltreatment. Nobody believed the excuse. The workers ignored the suggestive reticence of their leaders and the risk of a forbidden demonstration. It was estimated that five to six thousand came to the funeral. Not a single one of the official Party leaders was among them.

The editor of the literary section of the *Rote Fahne* wrote to me: '. . . if you should find it too hard to bear, remember the unforgettable smile with which your husband himself treated such behaviour.'

20.

Disintegration of the Party

There was nothing to keep me in Germany now. To me, Russia was no longer the paradise of the middle twenties, but even after my last visit and anxiety about new developments, there was still enough to attract me, particularly the human element. I was receiving many letters from Russian friends who, despite Stalin's mounting terror, showed more courage than my German comrades.

But there were still several months before I could travel to Russia. Pieck rang up to say that the Party would allow me one monthly payment in addition to the one provided by the Prussian Diet. I was still too ill to work. Eberlein advised me to discuss my future with Thaelmann: 'Write to him, he knows of your illness. After all, you were also the wife of Leviné. The Party has some responsibilities towards you.' But Thaelmann never received me.

My large flat was a good source of income. Three rooms were occupied by young Russian technicians, whose visitors provided me with another insight into the conditions and mood of the Soviet Union. I learned how Russia was dealing with the shortage of skilled agronomists: 'We let them loose as soon as they are able to understand their textbooks; they will learn.' As I was unable to hide my astonishment, I was told: 'You westerners will never understand. We cannot wait, we *need* agronomists now, so what should we do?'

The technicians themselves gave me hope. Raised under the new regime, they were ardently devoted to their country. Each of them, blissfully devoid of manners or traditions, looked ten years older when speaking of his work.

But my hope was soon shattered. The young enthusiasts were inspired by their leader, Ramzin, who was arrested and accused of subversive activity while his assistants were still living in my flat. A show-trial was to follow. Ramzin's lieutenants were deeply affected in a personal way: 'If Ramzin turns out a traitor, we cannot trust anyone, wife, father or mother.' They grew apathetic. What is the good of work if it can be put to the advantage of our enemies or made useless by sabotage? But they never questioned the accusation. They had to believe in Ramzin's guilt because their own security depended on that belief. My lodgers now yearned for the security of their homeland, and literally counted the days until their return.

Ramzin had been 'unmasked' through his connections with the capitalist world. At his trial he confessed to crimes invented by the prosecutors, as did all the other accused. But there were no death sentences. Months later, when I was in Moscow, I discovered that he had already been reinstated in his former position, which clearly made a mockery of all the accusations.

Someone in the Party found me a job collecting data for articles and treatises in the propaganda department. I had been spoiled with Ernst at my side as a constant source of information. Now that I had to fend for myself, I felt the discrepancy between my political experience, acquired in long years of communications with Party leaders, and my theoretical knowledge. In the past, I had not participated in current Party affairs, did not repeat its slogans and instructions, but now, eye to eye with various leaders, I made no secret of my objections and on occasions very passionately defended my views. But I understood that the place for criticism was the Party cell and not in private conversations.

Our entire propaganda concentrated on war scare and vilification of the 'social-fascists', a pattern set by the last Party Congress of 1929. Remmele thundered: 'All signs point irrevocably to the fact that war now stands on the agenda of history: war waged by the big capitalist powers against the Soviet Union. And the basic assessment by the VIth Congress of the transformation which took place afterwards proved correct: it is the SPD and the Second International which stand today at the head of the ideological preparation of the war against the Soviet Union . . . The social fascists are the keenest champions of fascist terror against the working class, within and outside the Government.' For good measure he declared that the SPD was also a completely bourgeois party in composition and that the 'Left' social-democrats were a thousand times more dangerous to the revolution than the 'Rights'.

On the other side, Thaelmann himself explained that the social-democrats were still in possession of the decisive mass-basis within the worker ranks. But flagrant contradictions were ignored and propaganda methods grew coarser almost daily. And yet our Party cell took everything in its stride. Not a word, not a gesture, not a raised brow betrayed the slightest disagreement. Any appeal to sanity on my part would have been a cry in the wilderness.

The new line was firmly established but occasions were bound to arise which would allow for some cautious remarks as a start. I was a novice and, after four years absence from Party work, I needed to gain some confidence.

I hoped to win over some more sophisticated Party members and had a good opportunity with Romma, a Polish woman who lived in my flat. In the course of their political life, she and her husband sometimes came in conflict with the Party line. But in those faraway days it did not affect their esteem nor their positions in the Party. It was different now. Her husband had staunchly rejected the term 'social-fascism' and was detained in Moscow. She somehow escaped the net and was sent to work in Germany. During this time we had many conversations in my kitchen, and I could see she was suffering from the separation with her husband.

Soon Romma left for Moscow to give an oral report to the Comintern and to see her husband. She was quite determined to back him now more explicitly, whatever the cost to her own position. But she found he had undergone great changes and was conditioning himself to accept the current Party line. He accused her of having been infected by my opportunism and lack of revolutionary spirit. They quarrelled incessantly; in the end he hardly spoke to her at all.

On her return, we both tried to explain her husband's attitude. What made him change? Of course, she wouldn't admit any personal weakness. Bukharin's capitulation was complete. Not a word of discord in the entire press. The Comintern raved of an approaching revolution. There was no time for discussions – should he watch events from outside the Party when unity was more necessary than ever? 'Russia is in danger, we cannot let her down now.'

And what could Romma herself do outside the Party? All ties with her former life were broken, she had no profession, she lived on false documents provided by the Comintern. Her marriage itself was at stake. It was easier to swallow one by one the perilous Party slogans and pretend she was doing it for the revolution. The flat resounded with her passionate outbursts against my opportunism. All arguments were lost on her. I showed her an absurd article which claimed: 'We must first of all make clear to the Social Democratic workers that what we have now is fascist dictatorship and we must not, therefore, wait for any decisive fights in future.' She answered me by referring to Thaelmann's admonition of those who were 'indulging in minute calculations of percentages and degrees of German fascism', which he contemptuously called 'steps-theories'. This was early 1932. Kirov, Zinoviev's successor as head of the Leningrad Soviet, resolutely declared that German fascism had reached the ominous figure of 96 per cent. Who could care about the remaining 4 per cent?

I asked her who was carrying out the fascist dictatorship in Germany, and read her Thaelmann's speech of February 1932: '. . . In pursuing its fascist course, the present policy of the German bourgeoisie is characterised by its unique alternative use of the Social Democratic Party and Hitler's Party, with the Social Democratic Party still functioning as the principal social prop for the bourgeoisie. The Centre is momentarily the party which is drawn into the foreground by finance capital: at the present time finance capital's policy is being carried out by the Centre together with Social Democracy.'

This implied that the Centre was carrying out the fascist dictatorship. 'Well', she said, 'we all know that Thaelmann is not much of a theorist.'

'What about the intelligent workers we are supposed to win over? We make ourselves a laughing stock.'

'No one takes the press seriously.'

The Russians were progessively confusing pro- and post-revolutionary tasks. On the Russian agenda stood the building of feeding centres for the workers, and in 1932 Piatnitsky set the German Communists the task of doing the same for the German unemployed. Our wretched rank and file were ordered to collect donations. They felt it was an impossible task and grumbled on the quiet. But Romma was unmoved: 'The workers cannot fight on an empty stomach – we must first feed them.'

'The Bolsheviks only set themselves the task of feeding the workers *after* the Revolution, when they became the state. We are only relieving the bourgeoisie of their obligations', I said. 'It is different in Germany', was her answer.

No Party absurdity was too big for her to swallow. The fiasco of the Presidential elections of 1932 was explained in the following terms: 'The Party failed to put into the centre of our election-campaign the fact that the Imperialist war has already started, and the acute danger of an intervention against the Soviet Union is becoming more real. We were not able . . . to successfully arouse and organise a concrete mass-resistance against the delivery of ammunition supplies.'

'We cannot speak enough of the danger, the more the better', she remarked.

It took some time for Romma's husband to take the final plunge, to write an article in defence of the slogan 'social fascism', which appeared in the summer of 1932. In it he drew a picture of the 'final' transformation of the SPD into Social Fascists.

'It was necessary', Romma said. 'The Workers will soon understand the counter-revolutionary role of the SPD – a bit of exaggeration does not matter'.

The husband was now considered fit for Comintern work and soon arrived in Berlin. But he quickly realised what the new policy had done to the Party; its faked successes, its impotence in spite of the impressive membership. He was utterly shaken: 'I was wrong, we must warn, cry out, I must disclaim my article, set an example. It is my duty to the revolution.'

It was Romma who held him back: 'And who will trust and follow you? Who will take you seriously now?'

In the summer of 1932, Anna Pankratova arrived and the two temperamental ladies allied to fight against my 'opportunism'. Our discussions reached a climax during the presidential elections. The Party had again put up Thaelmann as its independent candidate. The resulting election of the monarchist Hindenburg might have been avoided by the building of a united front with the SPD. A similar situation had occurred under Ruth Fischer's leadership, and she was attacked for it by the Comintern.

'A united front with Social-Fascists? You call this a Left Block?', cried the ladies.

'The Party was criticised for this attitude before; we cannot make the same mistake twice', I argued.

'It is different now, after the Social-Democrats became Social-Fascists in earnest.'

'You gave them the name, not the millions of workers and other prospective voters. We must offer to support their candidate under conditions carefully devised and popular with the masses. This was the course advocated by the Comintern, I am repeating what I was taught and just refuse to forget.'

'We cannot sit with Social-Fascists at the same table, it is gross opportunism.' I reminded them that Lenin said we should sit even in a pigsty if necessary for the revolution.

Suddenly there was a slight change in Romma's attitude to me: 'What is the Central Committee going to do for you in case of Hitler's victory? Have they provided you with safe quarters and ap-

propriate documents ? You could not live under your name.' The
reason for her change was another shift in Party tactics. One evening she remarked: 'You were right about the presidency. Pieck offered to support an SPD candidate even without any conditions at
all.'

'Well, Romma, what are you going to do now ? You called
my idea "gross opportunism" – are you going into opposition ?' She
broke down and said in desperation: 'What gives that man such
power over us ? What makes us submit to a policy which we know is
leading to disaster ?' 'That man' was Stalin.

Alone with me, Romma now permitted herself to criticise.
When Pankratova, on the evidence of official data, denied that the
Party was responsible for splitting the trade unions, Romma said
bitterly: 'Only a short while ago she would have laughed in the face
of such informants.'

But Romma herself was one of them. She wrote passionate
articles in defence of our trade-union policy, distinguished herself
as a delegate at various Congresses and was acclaimed for her devoted work. She moved away and I don't know whether she and her
husband were both liquidated in spite of their faithful services.

As for myself, I tried to dodge responsibility by working exclusively for the Russian propaganda section. Hard work helped to
overcome suicidal spells; clever Pankratova waived off the idea:
'You won't find the time for it.' I was rooted in the Party though
everything revolted me.

Ernst used to say that the surest sign of disintegration is corruption at the top, and I had the dubious privilege of watching the
mood, language, personal relations, cynicism of the leaders – everything indicated a sorrowful decline. One Saturday I
came to collect my wages and it appeared that someone had forgotten to leave an order.

'Those creatures !' screamed the Chief of our Financial Department, 'You are doing all the work for them, they only scribble

some rubbishy sentences, sign their names and pocket the money. It is sheer exploitation and they haven't even the decency to write out an order in time.'

'They' meant, in this case, Comrade Lenz, the head of our Propaganda Section and member of the Politbureau. He himself was a member of the Central Committee and of the Prussian Diet. To all intents and purposes, I was an outsider, not exactly popular with the clique.

Corruption was felt in every corner. One morning Frau Stoecker rang me up. She and her husband were going as guests to a holiday resort in the Crimea, and she wanted to know what objects to buy for resale to the Russian comrades. 'You intend to do business with people who are your hosts ?', I asked.

'But they all do it. All my husband's colleagues. The Russian comrades are delighted to get some of our products and they have plenty of money, with nowhere to spend it.'

Another symptom was the alarming spread of sexual promiscuity in the last pre-Hitlerian years. Radek once told me that contrary to all gossip and rumours, the first few years of the Revolution were marked by great sexual restraint, particularly within the Party. 'This', he explained, 'is another proof of the sanity of our Revolution. It is still in the ascendancy and we are too absorbed in the fulfilment of our great tasks.' The conclusion was obvious: a well functioning Party would be 'too absorbed' at such a crucial time to indulge in an excess of sexual activity.

Opposition to the Party in Germany ceased to be only a struggle over political views. In most cases it meant the loss of livelihood – particularly menacing in the face of growing unemployment. Abuse and vilification were painful enough, but above all was the threat of banishment from paradise. 'I cannot cut myself off from the Soviet Union', was the most repeated argument.

This state of affairs led to shameless acts of capitulation. On 23 February 1930, Arthur Ewert, a leading member of Ernst's faction, wrote an open letter in *Rote Fahne* to The Secretariat of the Central Committee:

Dear Comrades,

The increasingly critical political situation in Germany, the increased tightening of the united front of all reactionary forces, including the SPD, against the Communist Party, and the growing threat of war against the Soviet Union demands from every Party member an unequivocal attitude towards the policy of the Comintern. Since, up to the Wedding Congress, I advocated views which were at variance with key decisions of the Comintern and the KPD on a number of issues, I would now like to make the following statement:

I acknowledge that the views which I defended until the Wedding Congress, and which were rejected and fought against by the Party, were incorrect. My assessment of the situation proved wrong. The crisis in the United States and above all the worsening of conditions in Germany have confirmed the views of the Comintern and the Communist Party. The same also applies to the tactical questions on which I opposed Party resolutions (trade unions, elections of factory councils, social fascism).

I pledge myself to actively carry out all Party decisions and recognise the inadmissibility of building any factions or groups.

I am in complete agreement with the general line and the tactics of the Central Committee of the Soviet Communist Party and reject the views represented by Comrade Bukharin.

I pledge myself to fight under the guidance of the Central Committee and its leaders against all opportunistic notions within the Party, the enemies of Brandler's organisation as well as any conciliatory attitude towards them.

My agreement with the decisions of the Comintern and the Party and my pledge to actively carry them out also extends to the resolution of the Comintern concerning the Wittorf affair.

With comradely greetings

signed: Arthur Ewert

Heinz Neumann's wife gives an excellent picture of the unfortunate Communist leaders, manipulated by the Comintern during this period. Speaking from close observation of her own husband, she concludes:

'In his dependence on his masters he fails to speak his mind freely, his confidence in his political judgement is, therefore, shaken and, consequently, his capacity for critical evaluation . . . He starts by suppressing criticism for the sake of "solidarity with the movement" but the boundaries get confused in the process of mutely accepting commands. In constant conflict with himself, he eventually becomes a prisoner of the Party and Comintern apparatus. In the end, put through the grinder of criticism and self-criticism and forced to deliver public confessions – against his convictions – of alleged political mistakes, his spiritual backbone is soon broken.'

Unfortunately, Heinz Neumann, was not one of the passive sufferers at the hands of the Comintern. He himself played a prominent part in crushing backbones, and often by very ugly methods. But this does not change the validity of his wife's picture. Neither is the suffering of the unfortunate Neumann, himself a victim of Ruth Fischer's practices, to be questioned when he received a taste of his own medicine.

I remember Ernst's words on hearing of Bukharin's first capitulation in November, 1929: 'If they only have room for crushed personalities, there is historically no longer any room for a Communist Party.'

21.

Russia, 1931

I now concentrated my Party work on Soviet Russia and in 1931 decided to have another look at it. I also wanted to ensure the publication of Ernst's book on the Spartakus League, which the German Party had refused to publish. I hoped the Russians would be more objective.

Upon arrival in Moscow I immediately visited Radek who, after his capitulation, was assigned the editorship of *Isvestia* and was rumoured to be Stalin's chief advisor. I heard from reliable Party sources that he had been brought down by an internal ailment directly affecting his sight. A prolonged exile under unfavourable climatic conditions would threaten him with complete blindness. But his capitulation was received in a spirit of forgiveness, he was allowed 'extenuating circumstances'. He was not reinstated in his former Kremlin dwellings but lived in his wife's flat. She had retained her own position – at that time families were not yet automatically punished for the sins of their relations.

I found him a little subdued but still bristling with wit and energy. He thanked me for entrusting him with the publication of Ernst's book: 'I promise to treat it as carefully as I would wish my own works treated when I am gone. I had many controversies with your husband but I know how to respect a man of Ernst Meyer's value. Of course it will be published, no one could be better suited for this job.' He offered me work in his forthcoming monthly periodical *Behind the Frontier*. I was to write articles and find other collaborators. He then asked me about conditions in Germany. I answered: 'This is my firm conviction: if there are other ways of achieving a revolution than those shown by Lenin we shall have it within a maximum of two to three years. If not, we are irretrievably lost.'

At that moment, Preobrazhensky entered the room. Radek introduced me: 'Meet Comrade Leviné, just arrived from Germany', adding in his usual jocular way: 'You know, she is very smart, she wants us to do the job for the German Party and bring them the Revolution on the bayonets of our Red Army.' I exploded: 'Not I, but the Comintern, which makes a mockery of Lenin's teaching, seems to rely on the Red Army instead of the German Party. You must do something to prevent impending catastrophe. It is your responsibility, think what history will say of you.' Radek shrugged his shoulders and said: 'Who cares for history, we shall all be dead by then.' Preobrazhensky made no comment.

I showed him some examples of working-class 'menus' I had collected to demonstrate at meetings the plight of the German unemployed. He laughed: 'You mean to impress our audiences? No, this is not good enough, or bad enough, whichever you like. Better not speak of it.'

I asked, in my turn, how things stood in Russia, how long would the hardships last? He confidently assured me that the worst was past. Another year perhaps and the benefits of the Five-Year Plan would be seen – its success was unquestionable, he said. But he was indignant about the Party's tales of Russia's life of plenty: 'It is utterly wrong. On the contrary, Russia's difficulties should be made known to arouse class solidarity for the revolutionary workers and urge them to come at long last to her aid. Truth is, in this case, a matter of revolutionary expediency. Your methods breed passivity: they sit tight and wait for powerful Russia to come to *their* aid.'

I was shocked by the changes which had taken place since my last visit, only two and a half years before. But I had every reason to believe Radek's assurances that the peak of the calamity was past. My visit coincided with the announcement of Stalin's famous 'six conditions' – differential pay rates, personal managerial responsibility, greater attention to the needs of the old technical cadres and so on. The points which made everybody heave a sigh of relief were generous promises of improved living and working conditions.

So the Five-Year Plan started bearing fruit and Stalin's prestige was rising by leaps and bounds. Everybody spoke of the 'wise, great realist', 'the down to earth ruler', who knew exactly what the country needed.

I watched Stalin's methods in practice. First of all the working class was split into various sections, according to their value to the industry. A kind of 'workers' aristocracy' was created in the section indispensable for the main work. These workers were given preferential food and payment, were fêted and flattered. When decrees were introduced punishing a single day's absenteeism or change of working place, by loss of ration-cards or eviction, the privileged were reassured: 'The decree does not apply to you. You don't belong to the despicable category of idlers and careerists looking out only for themselves. You have set out to fulfil a historic task, the world looks up to you in admiration – you need not worry.'

And the Party, formerly so proud of its exclusiveness and wary of becoming submerged in the backward, unenlightened masses, now sought new members without discrimination. Rosa, Jaglom's wife, belonged to a commission interviewing prospective members, and I was permitted to attend one of their sessions. A young worker appeared.

'Who is Stalin?'

'The Leader.'

'But what is his job? In what capacity does he lead?'

'As a leader.'

'Don't you know that he is the General Secretary of the Party?'

'Oh yes, he is the greatest of them all, the General.'

Her charitable hint misfired, she was getting nowhere and switched to another subject: 'What do you know about the Opposi-

tion and Bukharin?' His face was blank. Another member cautioned: 'The question is too generally stated.' Rosa corrected herself: 'Tell us something about Bukharin's fight against the Party.'
At last the worker became quite articulate. He had heard plenty of
speeches at his factory meetings: 'Bukharin is helping the Kulaks
and the NEP-men. He is harmful to the Party. We must fight him
with all our might.' He was admitted to the Party by virtue of being
'an honest proletarian'.

The period was remarkable for the cynicism of the ruling
circles. They mocked at the promises of the Five-Year Plan and circulated bitter jokes: 'Two friends meet in the air – of course ordinary means of communication will soon be a thing of the
past – "Where are you flying to?" The friend names a remote pro-
vincial town.

"What for?"

"It is rumoured that they are distributing ¼lb of butter on
last year's ration-card." '

To cope with the catastrophic meat shortage, the planners
launched an extensive campaign for breeding rabbits. The papers
devoted pages of instructions, incentives and praise of successful
breeders.

'What is a rabbit?' asks a Comrade.

'Don't you know? The Cattle of Comrade Stalin.'

Or: a bewildered Molotov says to Stalin:

'I was looking everywhere for the new Giant-Provision
Store announced in *Isvestia* and couldn't find it.'

'You'd better stop looking and stick to the papers. It is all
in there.'

The Soviet government appealed for a loan. The first response came, naturally, from the factories with the largest Communist cells. To set an example, they donated a month's wages and
more. 'A socialist competition' encouraged the workers to contribute even more. The response was overwhelming, with offers pouring in from institutions, schools, individuals – who would have the

courage to abstain? A local branch of Soviet bureaucracy had its hands full registering contributions. They seemed baffled by the power of their 'persuasion', giggled and made sarcastic remarks: 'Look at those enthusiasts! They just cannot wait to part with their money.'

I arrived in Moscow at the close of the so-called 'Menshevik Trial'. Not for a moment did my Russian friends doubt the fantastic indictments. Pankratova gave me a detailed account of the proceedings, disclosing confidential facts, unknown to the public. She insisted on my reading some of the more compromising documents. It was obviously not so much her desire to convince me – it did not occur to her that I could doubt – as her urge to share a shattering experience with me. I listened to her, read the many pages of accusations, it was all there, all well documented, and not for a moment did I believe a word of it. I was shaken and decided then and there never to live in Russia as long as such trials could take place. But I was still a 'believer' of a kind, still firmly convinced these were the last convulsions of a great upheaval and would disappear with the stabilisation which was now round the corner.

I thought I could turn my mind to the bright side of Soviet life and visited factories, schools, prisons. The country was still bristling with originality and initiative. I saw prisons where farmers were allowed three months leave of absence for seasonal work, and somehow never failed to return; where shows were staged at least once a month with prominent artists, including the ballerina Geltzer and the actor Neshdanov; where criminals were not punished but successfully reformed; where prostitutes were rehabilitated and lived a normal life. Prisons competed with factories for greater productivity and one of them topped the work norm and beat a Moscow factory for the trophy – a bust of Lenin. Houses for mothers and children were set up in all big cities as well as societies for child welfare. Factories sponsored kindergartens and schools, and young pioneers assisted in obliterating illiteracy and setting hygienic standards. Factories and pioneers had their own papers, young workers their own theatres, and the former pariahs of the country, the farmers, a paper with a circulation of 2½ million. Every large plant had its own literary circle and shock brigades of workers were attached to the Ministry of Education. I heard sentimental little tales of pioneers clearing up the ravages of the bitter past.

I visited Bolshevo, the colony for hardened criminals – including a number of murderers – and learned of their petition to the government to grant the head of the State Police, Menshinsky, Jagoda, his Deputy, and a number of Lieutenants, the Order of Lenin, the highest distinction of the Soviet Union, 'for working towards our transformation'.

Stalin's 'six conditions' sparked a campaign for bettering sanitary conditions, cleaning, beautifying, as if to give the promised bright future a worthy reception. The entire population, workers, housewives, adolescents and pioneers, were mobilised to inspect barracks, houses, feeding centres. In Moscow more trees were planted than had been for the last fifty years. The upsurge of energy and enthusiasm seemed to belie Trotsky's talk of apathy and indifference by which he explained Stalin's ascendance to power.

I was sent on a holiday. The place, chosen for me by the head of Stalin's Secretariat, was a former estate of Count Barjatinsky which had been turned into a rest-home. It was situated in the Kursk district, notorious for frequent draughts and spells of acute famine. The estate comprised several buildings and 150 rooms, complete with a magnificent 'English Park', fishing and bathing ponds, hot-houses and so on. Before the Revolution, hundreds of servants were permanently kept to maintain the place, which was visited once in two or three years for some odd weeks. Now about 200 people could recuperate there and restore their health. The house was packed with people working themselves to death to create better conditions, many of them bearing heavy scars from the civil war. 'Barjatinskoje' seemed a living illustration of social justice.

If, as could be hoped from Radek's statement and Stalin's promises, the end of hardship was in sight, the benefits would perhaps outweigh the great sacrifices. The Five-Year Plan was presented to the world as a conscious resolution of the proletariat to tighten, for a short while, their belts – as far as belt tightening was admitted at all – to achieve something of lasting importance. I knew better. I knew the workers had been tricked into the venture. But I was used to the idea that the Party, as the advanced section of the proletariat, was fulfilling for them not so much their actual, but rather their 'historic will'.

With this conviction, I returned to Germany as a reporter on Russian affairs. My chief exploit during that phase is documented in a twenty-four page article on 'The Importance of the Five-Year Plan'. It was ordered by our propaganda department as a guide for Communist campaigners in one of the forthcoming elections. In it I told of the great achievements of the Plan, using the evidence of official statistics – twenty-four pages of lies which read in retrospect like the ravings of a lunatic. I did it in good faith, particularly when describing the benefits awaiting the country in the approaching year of 1932. I also included, albeit on the insistence of Party authorities, passages about the great harm inflicted by the sabotage of the Kulaks and the old technical staff. It was amazing what I could do with a tiny twist of conscience, telling myself that, after all, the Kulaks *did* play a damaging part in the food calamity and there was an undeniable *tendency* among a section of the deprived leading technologists to boycott the new regime.

I regard these passages among my darkest mistakes and think that half-truth is the greatest lie of all. At meetings I resolutely refused to repeat the Party's tales of Russia's prosperous life, earning myself angry rebuffs from the respective chairmen. But the audiences were not really deceived by the Party, and I knew this from the thanks which even my half-truths brought me – they appreciated that I was not altogether intent on hoodwinking them.

I think my behaviour was typical of many 'honest Communists', fascinated by Russia's achievements and aspirations, who sincerely regarded the current defects as mere clouds in essentially sparkling blue skies. Another reason was lack of knowledge of what was really going on in the Soviet Union. It is futile to expect judgement on matters which one cannot verify by one's personal observations. This might serve as an excuse for the many sincere, intelligent, educated people who accepted Stalin's crimes with relative ease. Lack of information blurred their judgement and also made it possible to drown their consciences.

Many Party members continued to deceive themselves by justifying their capitulation, thereby ending any hope of opposition and leading to the final collapse of the German Party. For the first time in recent history, an opposition faced persecution by a revolutionary state, struggling not only against the national organisations but also against the Comintern, fortified by the power of the state machine.

Under certain conditions it was permissible for the opposition to refrain from *public* criticism and submit to the will of the majority, allowing it to test its policy in action. They could appreciate the force of circumstance and yet wait to throw themselves into the breach at the right moment. An opposition is not dead if it keeps silent for a while. Keenly aware of this, Stalin introduced new rules, demanded recantations and explicit declarations that the Party was right and oneself wrong. This kind of 'disarmament' (a key word in Stalin's political vocabulary) destroyed the flower of Russia's revolutionary leadership even before they were physically liquidated. It also crushed an entire generation of talented, devoted German leaders, thus aiding the rise of Hitler.

I assume that none of those who surrendered admitted even to himself that he was too weak to face the difficulties and too selfish to put the interest of the revolution above his own. I heard all the excuses and knew them almost by heart. They began by finding some merit in every new Party line, argued the necessity for giving it a fair chance to get going; there was the very laudable wish to 'serve the revolution under any circumstance', to 'stand by it at all costs'. Another common excuse was that submission was only temporary, with the option of disagreeing at a more favourable time.

There was another, more decisive factor: a revolutionary

caught and imprisoned by tsarist police might count on the help and sympathy of his friends and associates. But an oppositionist caught in Stalin's net suffered total isolation and a campaign of slander and abuse. This factor compelled me to make a desperate rush from the Soviet Union in early 1933, to the inevitability of a Nazi Germany. They did not yet shoot at us in Soviet Russia, but I felt I would not be able to efface myself so completely as to avoid prison or banishment. It was easier and more honourable to accept persecution from Hitler amidst sympathetic friends than from Stalin. I returned to Germany four days before Hitler became Chancellor, even with the risk of being arrested at the frontier.

Despite the crushing of German Communism and the danger of the spread of Nazism, the dreadful capitulation to Stalin continued unabated, as I discovered when I went into exile in France. A truly pathetic fear of breaking ties with the Party – and the revolution – could be observed among the German emigres in Paris. Loneliness and *self-imposed* starvation through loss of the few wretched francs of Party relief was a hard prospect. I felt guilty for not speaking up in public and sounded opinion to see what support I could count on under what seemed much more favourable conditions. Many admitted in private conversation that the Party line was wrong, even absurd.

'Why don't you say it openly ? Let's make a stand. A strong opposition might tip the scales and save at least France from Germany's fate. What are you afraid of ? The Party may order you at any time to return to Germany to do illegal work which you yourself think will lead nowhere. Is it easier to face a concentration camp ?'

'It cannot be helped – it is the duty of a Communist.'

In this manner the Party helped to defeat itself internationally in the years leading up to the Second World War. The revolution which had turned tsarist Russia into the Soviet Union was now bankrupt, and the idea of world revolution had become fearful because of the Soviet failure. But in spite of its later distortions, Bolshevism *did* work in the first few years of its power, and against incredible odds. In Germany we failed after we stopped following its original lead.

I still believe in the Communist revolution. In the West where it is a problem of better distribution of wealth, it could be achieved without shedding a single drop of blood. But this can be done only by a *true* Communist Party – unlike the present one, 'Communist' in name only.

Appendix

Personal Sketches
of Revolutionary Leaders

Muenzenberg

I first met Muenzenberg in the summer of 1919, while recuperating in a Black Forest spa from an illness after Munich. He came to hold a meeting in the nearby industrial town (Schwenningen) embracing some 10,000 well organised workers, chiefly members of the SPD and USPD.

Muenzenberg was short, slender and boyish looking, but bristling with energy and the self confidence of a man who knows his own powers. He considered me first of all for my publicity value. We had hardly exchanged a few words before he exclaimed excitedly: 'I will announce on the posters that the widow of Leviné will be in the audience.'

'Don't', I warned, 'or I shall not come at all.' He shook his head in surprise: 'No ? At least I shall announce your presence from the platform.'

'I shall bluntly deny my identity.'

He looked very disappointed but had to give in.

His brilliant speech erased the unpleasant interlude. He became for me the man with the power to carry on the great work. To him I was a useful propaganda object – sufficient grounds for a good friendship.

The great publicity genius was not discouraged by my refusal to play my part in the small town. He could make more tempting offers. He planned a tour all over the country, which he believed could be extended outside Germany, with me as the star attraction. He thought it all out: 'What a sensation! We might even be invited to America – we would become world famous celebrities.' Of course, the great orator did not need my help. My presence was only to serve as a living monument to a tragic event. We were to cash in on my grief. But he knew no limits and it took him quite a while to become reconciled to my refusal. He meant so well, and perhaps also expected a prize for himself.

Muenzenberg became interested in social problems at a very early age, and joined the local Socialist Youth at the age of seventeen. He soon left his native Germany and went to Switzerland. This was the beginning of his startling development. The unskilled and almost illiterate labourer soon gained access to intellectual anarchist circles. They did not satisfy him and his passionate search for knowledge and guidance drove him to the Bolsheviks. Lenin himself became interested in him and took great pains to discipline his vague radical ideas. Muenzenberg, in his turn, fell under the spell of the great master and became his enthusiastic disciple and a keen propagandist of his teaching. He was then arrested for his radical propaganda, and in the end expelled from Switzerland as an undesirable foreigner.

Amidst all the turmoil and excessive work, Muenzenberg somehow succeeded in getting engaged to two girls at the same time. He told me that both 'fiancées' visited him in prison, and he even managed to involve the prison Governor in this complicated triangle. Muenzenberg was allowed to meet the girls in the Governor's quarters, at different times of course. It was quite a feat to avoid a collision since the Governor was very generous in permitting the visits. He himself favoured the blonde Adele.

For quite a time I was Muenzenberg's confidante. He would often come just to pour out his heart. He would hardly mention Adele, but spoke in raptures of Fanny, describe their wanderings in the mountains, and the great harmony of their souls. When he spent a few weeks in Russia, where domestic virtues did not count much, the scales definitely tipped in Fanny's favour. But around

1922 he told me that Adele had won the day. Fanny had had enough broken promises and walked out on him. He could not leave Adele, he explained; she would not survive it. I found out later that his choice was not such a noble sacrifice. He preferred the cosiness, care, all the little things that usually make a marriage work, and particularly the excellent food. I have never known anyone so obsessed with it. He sometimes took me out for a drive in the countryside, in borrowed cars, and there was hardly a cafe, inn or restaurant he could pass.

I was not only a confidante. Love or not (i rather opt for 'not'), he might have preferred me to both girls or at least would have included me in the triangle – what a catch! On my return to Berlin, I found a huge bunch of roses and was told that many had arrived before. He had also done his utmost to find out the date of my arrival.

The two girls did not prevent him from taking an interest in other women. He was attracted to a very pretty secretary, coveted by many a comrade who came to Moscow as delegates to the Second Congress of the Comintern. She rejected Muenzenberg's advances in favour of Ernst Meyer. Muenzenberg was full of venom, and it may have been the start of his hostility towards Ernst Meyer.

On his return from Moscow, he rushed straight from the train to describe to me Ernst's despicable bourgeois habits. They shared the same cabin. Muenzenberg was appalled by the care Ernst took of his body – even of his nails: 'Oh! All those brushes.'

It was summer 1920, the start of my own interest in Ernst and I nearly said, 'Thanks for the information, Willi Muenzenberg, it is alright with me.'

Muenzenberg was chosen to launch a campaign for aid for starving Russia, badly hit by the great famine in 1921. Lenin himself picked him out for the task, which of course was of no small help to Muenzenberg. He founded the International Worker's Relief which soon blossomed into a powerful institution. Donations poured in from all over the world. Millions passed through his hands. Everything from textiles and medicine to machines were shipped to Russia. Muenzenberg achieved his ambition to become a celebrity, and without my help – he was quite capable of going it alone.

His prominent position had not spoilt our friendship. I was attached to him. There was some similarity between us, no political background, nothing to fall back on. And Muenzenberg was not a man to give up easily. Even my marriage made no difference. 'Don't tell me that you are faithful to your husband,' he said once. He was disarmingly cheeky, but he got his answer: 'I didn't say anything. But must it be you, Willi Muenzenberg ?'

Muenzenberg never made the social grade and was uneasy in the company of his bourgeois associates. They naturally appreciated his gifts and position, but treated him with a touch of amusement and even condescension. I was rather 'presentable' and sometimes he invited me to help him entertain some 'distinguished personalities' – he felt more secure in my presence.

Our friendship came to an end around 1924, when Muenzenberg suddenly severed all his former political affiliations and went over to the so-called ultra-left. It is true that he was by no means the only leader who went that way. A few genuinely believed in the promises of quick results: the revolution was allegedly around the corner. With Muenzenberg it was sheer opportunism. And none of the dissenters baited their former associates with such violence. This was the start of his political corruption and we drifted apart. I was repelled by his dishonesty, and for him I lost my attraction as publicity.

I was then the wife of Ernst Meyer, the most ardent and articulate opponent of the Left. At our occasional meetings Muenzenberg was very provocative and rude. In the summer of 1925 we met in the lobby of the Prussian Diet at the Party Congress. The Left ruled supreme and kicking the opposition was a rewarding game. Ernst Meyer was entering the hall and Muenzenberg said with a malicious grin: 'Look, here comes the Ernst Meyer *faction*.' I hit back: 'To be sure, the first sign of his return to prominence will be you, Willi Muenzenberg, trotting behind him.' He must have remembered Ernst's role in the Party and in his own life and murmured: 'But I have worked already on his side.' He blushed when I answered, 'That was a different Muenzenberg. He is no more.'

My prophecy proved true to the letter, and much sooner than could have been expected. Only two months later, in early September the Party line took a new turn unmistakably in Ernst's favour. Everybody regarded him as the coming man, including Muenzenberg. He immediately started to overwhelm Ernst with alluring offers. Yet his approaches stopped just as abruptly when 'a new line' once more swept Ernst from his leading position. This time, Muenzenberg brought into the fight all the pent-up fury for his humiliation. He found a worthy ally in the very gifted Heinz Neumann who nursed similar grievances against Ernst. The crudest lies and distortions were fabricated to discredit the defeated enemy. At the end of 1929, shortly before Ernst's death, they started a campaign to efface even Ernst's revolutionary past. Muenzenberg and Neumann declared that Ernst, one of the first members of the Spartakus League and co-founder of the KPD, sided with the anti-Bolshevik Kautsky and Haase.

In February 1930 we ran into each other by chance and he greeted me with the words: 'You see, I have won.' Ernst would not rise to power again – he was already dead. This time there was no answer; words failed me. I never saw him again, but he was a prominent public figure, and I could follow his activity, development and his increasing moral decay. He eagerly followed the Party line, but it did not help him and in the end he was dropped. Later, when Hitler was approaching France, where Muenzenberg was in exile, he hanged himself.

Radek

I met Radek in December 1919 and had rather mixed initial feelings. He was the legendary man whom the Soviet Government thought fit to participate in the shaping of the German Communist movement – in my eyes a kind of demi-god. I had not forgotten, however, his rude treatment of Leviné. Eager to obtain more first-hand information of Russian affairs, Leviné tried to meet him, but was curtly refused any communication. It appeared tht his spectacular rise to prominence made Radek very suspicious. He was quick to attribute it to the obscure manipulations of an ambitious careerist. He thought it particularly inadmissible for Leviné, at that time almost an 'outsider' in his eyes, to represent the Spartakists at the forthcoming all-German Soviet Congress to which neither Karl Liebknecht nor Rosa Luxemburg received mandates, overlooking the fact that it was not Leviné's choosing.

I nevertheless wanted to see Radek. Leviné left an unpublished book (*People's Voices on War*) and, anxious to secure its success, I decided to ask Radek for an introduction.

Radek had just been released from prison. He was arrested in February 1919 soon after the debacle of the so-called Spartakus Week. A high price was offered for his capture but it was his secretary, a dedicated Communist, who caused his arrest. She often worked late hours, and to reassure her jealous boyfriend told him that she was working for the famous Radek. He was thrilled, and kept on telling his workmates 'if they only knew who his girl friend was working for!' One of them found out and informed the police.

But he could not leave Germany – there was no direct frontier between Germany and Russia at that time, and he had to wait until some transport arrangements could be made. Responsible for his safety the Government kept him under a kind of house arrest. Only a few Party members knew of his whereabouts and they kept, in their turn, a careful watch on his visitors. The immediate link was Maslow and it took some persuasion to make him introduce me. He thought it was selfish of me to steal Radek's precious time. But Radek received me immediately. The unhappy incident with Leviné disturbed him immensely. I had hardly entered the room when he said, with great emotion, that he welcomed the opportunity to tell someone so close to Leviné how much he regretted his misjudgment. He would never forgive himself for his folly which had prevented him from meeting one of the greatest revolutionaries of our time.

Radek was not alone. Karl Moore, a mixture of idealist and adventurer, a man of considerable wealth and allegedly of princely extraction was also present. He was happy to meet me as he wished to offer me financial security for the rest of my life. Radek jumped to his feet. 'Leviné's widow does not need private help. It will be the honourable duty of the Soviet Government to look after her.' He will take the matter into his own hands to secure a quick and satisfactory arrangement.

So far the Party was paying me Leviné's salary. Radek found out that they failed to increase my allowance to the amount of the other members of the Central Committee. He was livid: 'Leviné has done more for the revolution than all the rest of them. It is an insult to his memory.'

It was the start of a great friendship as well as my political training. For several weeks until Radek's departure I used to arrive every morning and stay until late in the evening. An array of people came to the house daily; representatives of parties and innumerable revolutionary groups came to query, to argue, to criticise, to learn.

And Radek talked. He talked incessantly, all day long, apparently hungry for communication after long imprisonment. Most of the time he paced up and down the room – perhaps a habit acquired in prison, springy, fiery, conjuring up an image of a new, unconquerable Napoleon. His wit, for which he was famous, lent additional power to his argument. He silenced them all.

Radek was a man in his middle thirties and had a reputation for ape-like ugliness. He might have earned it by the peculiar arrangement of his beard and whiskers which almost covered his thin face, and first struck one's eyes. The opinion was unanimous, confirmed by friend and foe in innumerable descriptions. I believe it was the verdict of men – hardly a woman of his close acquaintance would have endorsed it. He was slightly built, of over average height, with a beautiful forehead, large piercing eyes, behind thick glasses, and an expressive, sensual mouth. Forewarned and duly prejudiced I was not able to consider him ugly. The idea simply did not enter my head.

When we were alone he used to tell me anecdotes of the recent past and often gay and mischievous stories, emitting a spirit of unmatched comradeship and mutual trust. Amidst the grim battle those weavers of history sometimes behaved like children engaged in a dangerous game. How far they were from the ruthless, sinister plotters painted by their enemies.

During the great controversy over Brest-Litovsk, Radek turned up at a meeting with a large bundle of books he'd just got back from a friend. 'A fine time to read novels', mocked Lenin. Radek: 'Well I am going to fight you, and you would not shrink from locking me up. So I thought I had better provide myself with literature.' Lenin gave him a friendly pat on his back. 'I may, my pet, I may.' Both laughed heartily at the idea; it was regarded as a good joke.

He told me of a prank he played on Chicherin, so characteristic of the prevailing mood and of Radek himself. Chicherin was the only bachelor among the leaders and Radek persuaded the printers to insert a notice into a few copies of *Isvestia*: 'By order of the Central Committee Chicherin is commanded to find himself a wife without delay.' The copies were distributed among the staff of Chicherin's department and they watched him studying the paper, walking from place to place to examine the other copies and getting angrier and angrier. Radek then had mercy on him.

One of the stories makes nonsense of all the speculations about Lenin's 'bribery by the Kaiser', be it for the revolution, as some graciously excused, or for personal gain. Lenin was quite sick on the return journey to Russia and believed that some wine or alcohol would do him good. 'A pity that the Kaiser's millions could not buy us at least a drink', he said to Radek.

In his memoirs Radek relates a conversation between a Red Army soldier and a Polish soldier. The Pole was boasting of their national emblem – an eagle. 'And it is an eagle with two heads', he said proudly.

'But ours is a star. No eagle can match a star. No matter how many heads you stick on it, it still remains a beast, but a star shines over the whole world.'

Radek believed he overheard the conversation on his return journey; in fact he told me of it in Berlin. He undoubtedly mixed up the dates for I well remember how it impressed me and how I marvelled at the sentiment with which this sophisticated man relished such innocent tales.

He told me of the crisis which followed the attempt on Lenin's life. There was not much hope of his recovery and everyone considered Trotsky the legitimate successor. It was the time when Trotsky was thought Lenin's equal and was even said to 'outshine' him. Trotsky knew of the mood. In one of his most moving speeches he paid tribute to the master and modestly repudiated the idea of being on a par with him. There could not be another Lenin. Radek put so much of his emotion into relating the speech that he 'outshone' Trotsky – the powerful orator himself. I read it many years later and could not recapture the excitement produced by Radek's story.

Radek spoke of both leaders in the same breath and I believe he would have been at great difficulty to say who was superior at that time. But he often spoke of the strange emotional appeal

Lenin exercised on people in contrast to the cold Trotsky. The members of the Central Committee as a rule addressed each other in the intimate 'thee'. An exception was made for Lenin and Trotsky. A deep reverence, as well as Lenin's age, excluded familiarity. The younger Trotsky excluded it by his aloofness; they admired Trotsky but reserved their affection for Lenin. The cynical Radek passionately declared that he, like all Lenin's entourage would have gladly given his life to save him.

This set of proud, self-confident people, almost unreservedly accepted Lenin's superiority. In Radek's words: 'It is a quite natural reaction. We argued, fretted, hit out for quite a while. But when events prove you again and again in the wrong and Lenin in the right, you tend to refrain from pushing your points too far. You are more cautious. And Lenin makes submission easy, he never hurts our feelings. He treats us, whatever our mistakes, as equals. Good lord, he can chastise! But he builds us up as lavishly as he pulls us down. After he has finished with us we only feel that we can do better, and we strive to prove it.'

Radek belonged to a prosperous, progressive Jewish family. He never spoke of his formative years or influences except for one little episode. He was forced as a little boy to wear his elder sister's lace-trimmed knickers. He regarded this as a gross humiliation, and fought a stubborn war against the disgrace. Leaving for school, he would take off the knickers and hide them. One sad day the trick was revealed. He suddenly fell ill and was taken home. The doctor was called and they began undressing him to put him to bed. 'The knickers! They must not find out!' He struggled, went into hysterics, swore to get well, all he needed was just to be left alone – he begged in desperation. Of course the secret was revealed and the knickers were put away for good. Who knows how much the episode influenced his make up. He for one thought it important enough to describe the story with great emotion some thirty years later.

He started his political career at a very early age, and as a youth of barely twenty years occupied a prominent position on the staff of the highly reputable *Leipziger Volkszeitung*. He soon met his wife and it was at least on his side 'love at first sight'. She will be my wife, he vowed. She was beautiful, a year or two his senior, a medical student or graduate, self confident, mature in outlook, rebellious. At the time of their meeting she had already had a child – a boy – by another man. His intelligence and position made her overlook his age and immaturity, but they made themselves felt at every step when they set up house together. After a relatively short while she decided to leave him.

'I know you will be back – we are made for each other', he confidently declared – 'and I shall wait for you.'

Not for Radek the romanticism of a broken hearted youth lingering in solitude. He soon started living with another girl, a colleague, but he meticulously observed 'fair play'. He told her in advance that he was deeply in love with his wife. He regarded their parting as a short interlude and would rush back to her at the wave of her little finger. A year later she returned to him, and their marriage survived all the adversities of the life of a Russian revolutionary.

He did not believe in 'physical faithfulness', even if he made a distinction between men and women. Women, particularly those on a higher cultural level and refinement, as was his wife, were not fit for promiscuity. But she was free to live as she chose, and it would not make any difference to their relationship.

A nasty incident nearly wrecked his political life. He was accused of embezzling 300 marks – some £15 – from Party funds. The chief plaintiff was Leo Jogiches. Radek told me without any bitterness that Jogiches might have been prompted by a desire to rid himself, or the Party, of a troublesome opponent. Perhaps it was something in between. A hapless mistake, very probable in an underground movement which makes it quite impossible to keep documents and receipts, threw suspicion on the unfortunate Radek. The matter was cleared up in the end but Radek went through a terrible ordeal. The case became universally known, and some wit added a K, the initial of his first name, to his second one, making 'Kradek' a close resemblance to 'thief'.

His indifference to money could also have played a part in

the incident. During his stay in Berlin he received money from Russia. Through the favourable rate of exchange, he told me, the sum by far exceeded the intended allowance. It did not occur to him, however, to return the difference, but neither did he keep the money. He just gave it away to everybody who needed it.

Radek's wife stood up gallantly to this unique situation. He said he would hardly have survived without her loyalty. It made him feel vitally indebted to her, adding a strong element to cement their relationship. When I visited them in the Kremlin three years later at the end of 1922 they impressed me as a blissfully happy couple, very much in love. Which again did not mean that Radek was not true to his philosophy. Of course, he admitted, it was a dangerous game and on occasions he was carried further than he wished. But he kept a careful watch on himself, and was helped by the tact and perception of his wife. She always knew when he was in the throes of this kind of conflict, and helped to bring him to his senses and – back to her.

He was careful, he told me, never to exploit his position. He never entered any intimate relationship with a woman in any way dependent on him, or who might profit by the association. A most impressive example was his attitude to Ruth Fischer. He thought her very beautiful and talented, and spoke of her rapturously. She often visited him in prison, and everybody expected him to woo her when he was set free. He didn't. He went so far as never to see her alone. He was convinced that she would soon replace Rosa Luxemburg and considered it his task to assist and promote her as much as he could. Personal attachment would mar his intentions and harm the Party. It was a great sacrifice for a man like Radek.

He wasn't a great judge of men, and I was aware of it even at the time of my exalted admiration for him. And he knew nothing of me. My personal loss was also a loss for the Party, and his compassion for me was very real. He also greatly exaggerated my looks, and obviously enjoyed my company. There were moments when he must have felt more involved, and to work off such sentiments would start speaking of his wife, unmistakeably underlining her superiority over me. He generally did not think much of my intelligence. When he deigned to listen at all, he sometimes said: 'It was a clever observation. Were you aware of what you have just said, or was it only a chance remark?' He was obviously quite unaware of the rudeness of such questions. 'As you wish, Comrade Radek', I answered once. He was startled, and for a moment appeared to be put out by my irony, but was too absorbed in himself to understand my rebuke.

I knew only one conversationalist to match him, and that was Leviné. No less captivating, his conversation was distinguished by warmth and respect for the listener. It was only natural for me to make comparisons and to ask myself why, in spite of all my admiration and gratitude I could never fall in love with Radek. It was chiefly his self-absorption which excluded a stronger feeling on my part.

Needless to say that Radek dominated the German scene, with the Chief of Police as his obedient servant. Once he decided to take me to the theatre. Such outings were not on the Police Chief's list, but he did not so much as murmur a protest. To his horror Radek decided to walk to the theatre, another transgression. It was a long way but surprisingly no one spotted him. And he made himself quite conspicuous by loud talk and laughter. He was not very considerate in the theatre either. When it came to the sentence – the play was *Easter* by Strindberg – 'God provides for all living creatures' Radek shouted from our box: 'Oh yes? We know better!' The Chief of Police gasped; his wife, who was also invited, nearly fainted. It created quite a commotion in the theatre, but Radek was boisterous and uninhibited, like a child; he simply had to protest against such a provocative sentence, he said. The Chief heaved a sigh of relief when we returned safely home.

Radek was a great reader. In Germany where the newspapers carried daily instalments of novels, he swallowed them all, including detective thrillers of no great literary value.

I had the good fortune to meet Radek at his best. He left Russia steeped in the glory of its great achievement. He witnessed the fulfilment of the ideas to which he dedicated his life. He then spent many months in prison where he actually witnessed the murder of Leo Jogiches, one of the best leaders of the German Revolution, after the assassination of Karl Liebknecht and Rosa Luxemburg. It happened not far from his own cell. On several occasions he himself faced death, and it was in prison that he learned of the birth of his only child. These experiences made him shed many of his frailties. He was alert to human suffering and very compassionate, exercising an almost unlimited influence on people, including his jailors. The jailors spied for him, gave him timely hints of plots, warned him against taking his daily exercises when something was afoot, and thus actually saved his life. There were quite a few attempts by the early Nazis to take matters into their own hands, and rid the fatherland of dangerous men.

Radek always read his articles to me before releasing them for publication. He told me he needed a reader for testing his arguments and I was to serve as the guinea pig. He modestly accepted criticism and corrections. Neither his German nor his Russian was impeccable, as close to perfection as they were. He never failed to have his writing corrected however pressed for time. He was also uncertain about his Russian spelling and sometimes dictated his letters to me. It was always great fun. Even the official exchanges bore the mark of his peculiar wit. Referring to the secrecy with which the route of his return journey was treated, he dictated the following letter to Litvinov: 'No use applying contraceptives after pregnancy has taken place.' 'And why not ?' he said when I looked baffled, 'It best illustrates the point. The route has been common knowledge for quite a time.'

Between the moving anecdotes and occasionally not very edifying gossip about Kollontai's and Balabanova's love-lives he talked politics. During the Spartakus Week he sent a letter to the Central Committee warning against a premature uprising and predicting its doom. He was very proud of this 'historic document' and told me with delight one day that it was fortunately recovered. 'What should the Party do in Berlin ?' I wanted to know, but he never gave me an unequivocal answer. He praised Leviné's leadership as a 'classical example' and defended Paul Levi who had disagreed with Leviné. 'Levi cannot be trusted with the leadership of the Communist Party', I declared firmly. 'He is not a revolutionary. Some time or other he will show his cloven hoof.' My arguments must have sounded a bell in Radek's mind. He took me very seriously on this point: 'But what can we do? We cannot dispose of him, he is the best head the German Party was left with.'

'He must be removed', I insisted. Characteristic of my attitude which was shared by all I knew was the idea that it was entirely within Radek's power to remove any Party leader, and he had not repudiated this, or explained to me that the sole arbiter in such matters was, or must be, the Party. He knew very well that he could build up or demote a leader but it took quite a long time for the Comintern to make use of its dominant position.

I used to meet him quite regularly, either in Berlin or in Moscow. On my first visit to Soviet Russia, in September 1922, already married to Ernst Meyer, we ran into him in the street on the first day of our arrival. He solemnly congratulated me on my marriage. I protested: 'You could have done it long ago; my relationship with Ernst was known to you.'

'Before, it would have been an indiscretion; now it is a duty.' He always had the right answer.

As usual he had a story to tell. He was coming from the Kremlin, and had a talk with Lenin. It was the beginning of the New Economic Policy, and the first trade fair in Nizhni-Novgorod. Business was good, they wined and dined, and sent a telegram of thanks to 'our great, dear leader, Lenin'. Lenin found it rather difficult to swallow. He kept on scratching the back of his neck, and repeating: 'It's too much of a good thing, much too much.'

Radek's life in the Kremlin did not differ much from his life in Berlin, it was only far less comfortable. His three-roomed flat overflowed with books and manuscripts. It looked more like a preposterously untidy library than living quarters. Heaven only knew how he could ever find the necessary book; it must have been agony. But Radek was no exception. These were still the days when Party leaders observed Lenin's demand for restraint and austerity in their personal lives. In fact he demanded that the salary of the foremost leaders should not exceed that of a skilled factory worker.

It was my intimate knowledge of Radek which taught me that the politician cannot be separated from the man. Radek, the devoted revolutionary whose talents and scholarship easily matched the most prominent leaders, never achieved the stature of, say, Zinoviev, or Bukharin. He was to remain the sparkling pamphleteer. An innate streak of buffoonery undermined the great qualities of this unusual man. The Russians have a saying for it: 'For the sake of a good joke he would not spare his own father'.

In 1925 one of the Russian emissaries, Schubin, visited us in Berlin. Speculation arose about the replacement of Zinoviev whose pending removal from the Comintern was by then a foregone conclusion! Couldn't it be Radek? 'What! this buffoon!' (I used the Russian word, Petrushka) and Schubin exclaimed: 'How well you know . . .' – he quickly controlled himself – 'the Russian language'. He obviously wanted to say 'Radek'. But Schubin was a cautious man. He joined in our laughter though.

I saw Radek again in January 1933.

I had no more hope that Ernst's book would be published. (See Chapter 21.) In the summer of 1931 a letter from Stalin appeared in the *Proletarskaja Revoluzija* denouncing the German, in fact all Left groups, with the exception of the Bolsheviks, as weak, impotent, badly organised, ill equipped ideologically, complete with an attack on Rosa Luxemburg whose ideas were a deviation from Trotskyism – the avant-garde of the counter-revolutionary bourgeoisie. The letter unleashed a violent campaign against Luxemburgism. Radek was no exception: he quickly dissociated himself from Rosa Luxemburg, an admired friend. 'It was a historic necessity' he said to me. He still spoke in high-falutin phrases to cover his cowardice.

'In view of the new turn, there is of course no hope of publishing Ernst Meyer's book which recalls the heroic history of the Spartakists', I said.

'You are mistaken. Stalin himself said it must be published, only later.'

'Later' was no great comfort, but I thought I might persuade Radek to talk to Stalin about the German Party. Perhaps catastrophe could yet be averted. Even if Germany was lost other countries could be saved by a change of policy. It was worth trying.

Radek was living in the 'Government House', the craze of Moscow. It was described as an example of 'things to come'. Fairy tales were told about the dull building, where lifts were more often than not out of order, hot water not running, heating not functioning.

Radek let me in himself. He was nursing a pet in his arms. I strangely do not recall whether it was a dog or a monkey. Perhaps the monkey was just my own imagination. Radek began his customary buffoonery: 'Meet my best friend. I can speak to him about anything I like. I can confide in him implicitly, for he will never give me away.'

I was in no mood for jokes and he became serious. 'See, you were wrong about the German Party; it has been working splendidly. Six million votes in the last election and they achieved it by their own efforts, without any financial aid from us. I should know, I assure you.' I was beside myself: 'Be quiet. You forget what you yourself taught me; people give us their votes because we are "nice chaps". They appreciate our courage and devotion, but they still need the confidence that we can do the job, and this we have yet to prove. Our own Party members don't often answer our calls for strikes or even demonstrations because we have not proved that we are able to do it successfully. We do not need financial aid for elections, we have an army of tens of thousands of unemployed who made the revolution their profession and would do anything for the Party; for revolution is their last hope. All we have achieved is 6 million votes which we might lose tomorrow.'

Radek grew more and more apprehensive and asked in the end: 'What do you suggest?'

'Go to Stalin, you are his friend, he will listen to you. Go at once, and tell him all that I have told you.'

'I cannot do it, I have no influence at all; you are mistaken.'

'Then take me to Stalin, I will speak to him myself. I have enough evidence to make him shudder, and I am not scared.'

He considered for a moment.

'This too is impossible. I can do nothing, it is not within my power.'

No, he could not. I understood, it was already dangerous to be associated with somebody who was critical of the Party, which meant of Stalin. There was nothing more to say.

Stalin's letter created quite a commotion. A campaign against the Left – Rosa Luxemburg – while Hitler was already knocking at the doors could only be explained as a disguised initiation of a new policy. What else? There were quite a number of Party members and even leading functionaries who, on the quiet of course, despaired of the perilous Party line.

On the last visit Radek told me the real history of the letter. Stalin happened to be on holiday in the Caucasus. With more time on his hands, he came across an article of a certain Slutski who dared to claim that Lenin, the Bolsheviks, underestimated the danger of opportunism in the pre-war social democratic parties. Which means that Lenin was not at that time 'a true Bolshevik', Stalin commented. Such a sin could not be tolerated.

Stalin enquired: 'who is Slutski?' And people were at a loss, narrated Radek. 'They did not know what to say. Should they praise Slutski, or should they condemn him?'

He said it without comment. It was already natural for him that no-one should dare have an opinion of their own or to say something which Stalin would not like to hear.

I said goodbye, and carried away with me the memory of a crushed man, who could convey his inner thought only to the little animal in his arms.

Jakovin and Pankratova

Summer 1925 brought us into contact with a number of 'Red Professors' – an exclusively Soviet phenomenon – products of a scheme to replace quickly the old intellectual cadres. A careful selection was made amongst the best of the country's talent and revolutionary spirit and these were drilled mechanically to absorb in two years a curriculum normally designed for five. Why not? These people were used to performing miracles.

They had the best tutors. Lenin and Trotsky were themselves among the political lecturers. The first crop surpassed all expectations and later played a great part in the administration of their country. Some of them were singled out for further studies in Germany and they were as a rule better acquainted with the history of the German party, and Ernst's role in it, than our own circles. They came to seek advice and instruction.

Jakovin, who became a great friend of ours, was one of the Red Professors. He was married to a very remarkable woman, Anna Pankratova, who achieved considerable renown even outside Russia. Pankratova was in her middle twenties when I met her in Germany, rather plain, except for her penetrating, intelligent eyes. She was quiet and serene, and her ready subdued laughter put you at ease at once. She was a kind of legend, and I heard stories about her throughout Russia, in the Ukraine, Caucasus, Crimea. She joined the Bolsheviks in 1918 and organised clandestine Party work and guerrilla warfare against Denikin in 1919. She went for days without food or sleep; brief rests on the floor or table huddled in her sheepskin-coat for warmth, were her only relaxation.

Pankratova had two great loves: the Revolution and her husband – in that order. But she had a passion for friendship, rather than an abstract love for humanity. By profession a historian, she was chiefly concerned with the history of the labour movement and trade unions.

Jakovin eventually drifted to the Trotskyists although he had never espoused Trotsky's doctrines before. The trouble started when he ventured some criticism on matters of secondary importance. He was stunned at the rough rebuke. 'What? Are we not allowed to speak our minds? Are we to be turned into dumb conformists?' He became angry, sarcastic and provocative, and the rebukes grew into warnings. Then came *threats*.

'So Trotsky is right. You are out to stifle all Party democracy – long live Trotsky!'

Pankratova could not but agree with him about his right of criticism. She was only perhaps temperamentally opposed to any excess and was too cautious, which made him even more provocative. Gradually deprived of all his functions he was expelled from the Party and became a wanted man by the spring of 1928.

Judging from my own experience, the persecution of political rebels was not too harsh despite the outrageous treatment of Trotsky himself and of his closest supporters. The secret police were often disposed to turn a blind eye, and the Party as a whole was not at all in the mood to hunt non-conformists. So Jakovin continued to live in Moscow with frequent trips to Leningrad, where he stayed in the crowded flats of his friends. On many occasions he even stayed in his own apartment, which lay opposite the entrance of a long courtyard, and was shared by his furiously hostile mother-in-law, with friends and neighbours constantly popping in and out.

It goes without saying that Ernst and I received him as often as he chose to come. We lived in the rigidly guarded Hotel Lux, the headquarters of the foreign Communists, where no one was admitted without an identity-card. Jakovin had apparently got hold of a forged one. We went together to cinemas and for long walks in plain daylight. No one considered it his duty to turn him in. I was a little worried but Ernst commented: 'Let the GPU look for him, it is their affair.'

They 'found' him only when it became too dangerous to ignore him.

For a long time, Pankratova stood by him loyally. She supported him and his large family and visited him in exile. I should like to mention that as late as January 1933 it was not yet permissible to demand the desertion of a political outcast by his family. There was an outcry of indignation among my friends when zealous officials made such a suggestion to the young wife of an arrested Trotskyist. Pankratova took it upon herself to carry the case to some high authority.

Pankratova suffered beyond description. Her personal distress was aggravated by nagging doubts: 'What a waste of energy and strength! What a loss to the country!'

With the growing political pressure, her resistance began to fail. By 1931 something new had crept into her argument: 'He should sacrifice his grievances for the sake of the revolution.' I hoped it was only a slip of the tongue by a very tormented woman. She still spoke of opposition to wrong tactics and even made a promise: 'I am going to Germany soon, and shall make a thorough investigation. If your account is correct and your Party resolved to build separate trade unions, I shall fight. On this point no compromise is possible. I am too influenced by Lenin's teaching to permit such a flagrant error.'

When she came to Germany on a long study-visit in 1932, she was true to her promise to investigate the trade union situation. Who could supply better data than Fritz Heckert, the acknowledged expert and leader of that department? She devoted a full weekend at his home for discussions – she could do no more. She returned to me indignantly: there was not a shadow of truth in my accusations. Nobody ever thought of creating separate trade unions. 'You are on a dangerous path, it smacks of influence of the Right'. She repeated the arguments of the Party to justify the new creation of 'Red Trade Unions' – their existence could not be ignored. They were a mockery of Lenin's teaching which she knew so well – a few years ago she would have laughed at such 'explanations'. Now she did not want to face facts. And I was not yet able to face the fact that all was lost.

We had many violent encounters over the German party. The kitchen of my flat, my last in Germany, rang with her passionate defence of most flagrant errors and warnings against my 'opportunism'. She seemed so self-assured and confident. Nothing could shatter her beliefs. She silenced me in the end. I knew almost all her answers – they were printed daily in the *Rote Fahne* – what was the use of arguing ?

She had moved into a newly built house in Moscow – with no keys to the doors. She was sending some from Germany. But what of the other tenants of the large house who have no such opportunities and have to go out to work ?

'What a waste of energy ! How can they work with their mind on the unlocked doors ?'

'You don't understand us. You don't see the difficulties of our tasks. *We build with sacrifices comparable only to those of the ancient pyramid builders.*'

It was a terrifying confession ! Only a few years before the Pankratovas had prided themselves on building even without ruthless *modern* capitalist methods !

It would be difficult to assess the part, if any, the mounting political pressure played in her decision to give up her husband. I pleaded with her: 'Stand by him, wait. If I could only think of Ernst somewhere in the world I would have waited serenely for ever. Jakovin is alive.' I added my naive formula: 'Either the Five Year Plan will bring the expected results, in which case Stalin could allow some relaxation and a return to a normal political life, or it fails, and men like Jakovin will take their place with a changed leadership. It cannot last much longer.' It was summer 1931 and it seemed very logical.

She was in tears: 'We cannot go on. Politics is our life and we cannot bridge the chasm. My visits are sheer torture. On every occasion, amidst passionate kisses and caresses he is liable to say: If only you were not such a Stalinist. We are both too involved.'

Three years later, in 1934, she wrote nearly the same words to me in her parting letter from Paris, our last meeting place. But I would no longer vouch for the candour of her motives in dropping me as a friend. I suspected that she was afraid of an association with such an outspoken anti-Stalinist, who might come out in the open and even turn into a Trotskyist.

Bukharin

I first saw Bukharin in Vienna in the winter of 1913 / 14 at one of those affairs common to the Russian colonies abroad, literary and political lectures, discussions, occasionally even dances. There used to be quite a few striking faces in the audience, even Trotsky was sometimes present at those gatherings. But Bukharin stood out among them. There was in his appearance something of a saint, rather than a rebel. The image of Count Myshkin of Dostoievsky's *Idiot* involuntarily sprang into one's mind, at least the way the Russian actors tried to portray him. Perhaps this made me detect at once the humanitarian aspect of that unusual man. He was slightly built and looked even younger than his real age, only 26 at that time. His open face with the huge forehead and clear shining blue eyes seemed in its quiet sincerity almost ageless. We were never introduced and with all my hunger for new faces and people I never asked to be. I knew he was a revolutionary and saw no common ground for any relations between us. And he looked so remote like a star in the sky. One can admire stars from a distance.

We did meet though, and under quite unusual circumstances. One day I suddenly ran into him in the street when I was leaving the house. He hastily approached me, murmured 'Orlov', which was then his assumed name and without as much as greeting me, shaking hands by the Russian custom, asked: 'Would it be possible for you to lend me three crowns?'

Surprise and compassion made me speechless for a brief moment. I looked at him in horror and saw his pale face turn deep red with embarrassment. 'Of course, gladly'. I gave him the money. I would have given it at that moment, under any circumstances.

His face assumed its former paleness, he looked thin and very tired. Heaven knows how many days of starvation forced him to ask a stranger, for all he knew, a bourgeois girl, whom he had seen only at parties, for money. Three crowns was nearly the sum a 'gentleman-beggar' might expect as alms from any seemingly well-off person.

He ran away, sparing both of us any trite talk of returning the 'loan'. But after a few weeks he just as unexpectedly and abruptly gave me back the money. I might have been a bank clerk, the way he conducted the 'transaction'.

The second time – there was a second time – he shook hands with me and was more 'personal'. He even smiled and was bold enough to ask for five crowns. But he made no attempt at conversation; conventions seemed alien to his whole nature. The money was duly returned in the same way and place. He apparently lived in my immediate neighbourhood.

I met him again in Berlin in 1918 while working for the Soviet Embassy. I was not yet a Communist and got the job of interpreter on the recommendation of Karl Liebknecht's wife. One day, 'Orlov', the same unassuming, poorly dressed man passed through my office. I had a joyful sensation of meeting an old friend. He recognised me at once but was for some unknown reason frightened of being called 'Orlov'. Perhaps it was the old conspiratorial habit which he, like many others, had not shaken.

So that was the famous Bukharin of whom I had recently heard so much. To me he was still Count Myshkin and I was overjoyed when Frau Liebknecht called him so herself when we exchanged impressions.

Later on I eagerly followed his activities and read all his speeches and articles. Ernst Meyer, who came in closer contact with him, particularly during the second Comintern Congress in 1922, told me that Bukharin was very happily married, cheerful, witty

and – which seemed quite out of character – a great lover of ambiguous jokes and not so parlour-fitting language. I was surprised,
but not disappointed. Perhaps saints placed on earth need this
kind of balance. I learned that for several years he was on intimate
terms with Lenin and Krupskaya, the teacher and idol of the young
Communists and the darling of the Party.

Elevated to a position of power, Bukharin was utterly out of
his element and lost himself. Ernst Meyer had a taste of his devious
practices (see Chapter 12), but this did not prevent him from being
extremely friendly and helpful when we both came to Moscow in
the summer of 1928 for a long treatment of our respective turbercu-
loses. He visited us frequently, mobilised all the available
doctors – our quarters were simply invaded by them to Meyer's
annoyance –, made arrangements for our journey to the Crimea,
the best sanatorium, treatment and food.

He delighted my son of twelve and the boys who came to
visit him by his simple dress and unconventional manner. One of
them, a boy of 13 nearly broke into tears: 'Look how *our* ministers
behave, we will always be safe with such a government.'

Bukharin just looked a little bit better fed – no wonder after
so many years of dire privation – but still preserved his icon-like
face. Or had I not looked properly? For I was dismayed by his treatment of Trotsky and his handling of German affairs, to be sure, of
Meyer. I did not like him any longer.

I saw him for the last time in December 1928 in Moscow on
our way home. Together with Tomsky and Rykov he was then taking a firm stand against the initiation of the first Five-Year-Plan.
Bukharin visited Ernst once, but said that he would have to be more
careful to avoid a charge of factional activities in the International
as well. But he was in steady contact with Meyer through his lieutenants, particularly his devoted secretary Idolson.

Our room became a centre of the Russian opposition who
communicated all the details of the struggle. They were high-spi-

rited, full of pranks and jokes, confident of their victory. They described the proceedings of the Five-Year-Plan as a sort of stock exchange: everybody tried to outbid everyone else in quoting higher and higher figures. They were convinced that no one took the plan seriously in that form and that it was only a game to serve Stalin's dark purposes. Our quarters resounded with merriment and laughter and were christened by Bukharin 'The Inn of the Gay Conciliators'. (Ernst Meyer's faction had been suddenly advanced by the Comintern, from 'The Centre Group' to 'The Conciliators'.)

Bukharin seemed to be making a kind of moral come-back. It was puzzling though that his associates displayed much more courage than their master, an ill-omen in fact. No one wins a battle by carefully hiding behind the backs of others instead of leading. And a grim battle was in progress.

I never saw Bukharin again. But he went on sending Ernst his emissaries even after our return to Berlin, trying to raise an international opposition to do the job for him in his struggle against Stalin. It was a futile undertaking after having helped strangle the German opposition and raise Stalin's puppets to power. He wrote one memorable article though against the irresponsible, over-ambitious Five-Year-Planners. He put into it all the fire, erudition and power of persuasion left in him, to prove a simple fact, that one cannot build a house without basic materials. It was a heart-rending performance spoken with the tongue of an angel.

Bukharin later married the daughter of Larin, a young strikingly beautiful girl who could easily have been his daughter. A friend of mine who met him in Paris around 1935 and was not so harsh in her judgment as I was found him exceedingly charming, witty and happy in his young love. Apparently the laws of 'life goes on' also govern men like Bukharin.

I have never quite forgotten him. Everything connected with Russian music, writing, art, somehow conjures up Bukharin, who, more than any Bolshevik leader, valued them and was so utterly Russian. Bukharin, in his pathetic attempt to save some shreds of his personal and revolutionary honour at his trial, after throwing his whole personality to the wolves; Bukharin – battling for words, naively reminding his prosecutor Wyshinsky of a secret bargain allowing for some dignity, while proceeding to cover himself with eternal shame – was sometimes like a helpless, unjustly treated child. In the gallery of proud brilliant men, reduced at the trials to whimpering half-wits, disclaiming their glorious past and their very identities, Bukharin was the most tragic figure. He committed none of the crimes his executioners made him confess to. He was paying the penalty for the heaviest crime of all – for destroying, along with his life work, such a unique personality, the finest of its kind. There will never be another Bukharin in the world.

Index

Exclusive of Rosa Leviné-Meyer and KPD